# DESCENT
# INTO LIGHT

# DESCENT INTO LIGHT

## Dorothy Fielding

## BURNS & OATES

First published 1994
BURNS & OATES
Wellwood, North Farm Road,
Tunbridge Wells, Kent TN2 3DR

ISBN 0 86012 227 1

Typeset by Search Press Limited
Printed and bound in Great Britain by
Biddles Ltd, Guildford and King's Lynn

# Contents

# Foreword

## GERARD W. HUGHES, S.J.

This book is unique and original, simple and profound, earthy and mystical, written clearly, yet leading the reader into mystery, the mystery in which we all live and move and have our being.

Dorothy Fielding writes of her own experience of pain, rage, frustration, guilt and depression at her imprisonment from birth in a crippled body. In this imprisonment, she travelled painfully through the many layers of her consciousness, to an inner knowledge of her true identity. (Although very different in its details, the theme of the book is strikingly similar to Brian Keenan's *An Evil Cradling*.)

The importance, value and delight of Dorothy Fielding's book is that the identity she discovers is an identity in which we all share. Reading of her experience can help us glimpse, in the darkness and dread of things, the glory to which we are called.

There are statements in this book that may shock some readers at first. To take two examples: "I felt then that I was the Holy Eucharist, body and blood of the Living Christ" (ch. 6, p. 122). And, "I was a living part of every entity" (ch. 4, p. 97).

It is good to remember that classical spiritual writing contains many shocking statements, and also that what we think of as the normal world is, in fact, very mysterious. St Paul tells us that we are the Body of Christ. St Augustine, instructing his people on receiving the Eucharist, tells them to answer the priest's "This is the Body of Christ" with "I am." A modern nuclear physicist, writing of the ultimate constituents of our material world, states: "In every particle is contained every other particle."

For Dorothy Fielding, this journey through layers of consciousness took a form that was unique to her, vivid imaginative pictures at first, then later experiences so vivid that she had no need to record them and which had a lasting effect. It was only later that she discovered that what she was experiencing, while unique to her in its form and detail, was within a whole mystical tradition.

The details of Dorothy's imaginings and her way of describing them are unique to her and are relatively unimportant. She does not hold herself up as a model to be imitated, but simply relates her experience. She was led, very painfully, to an inner knowing, an inner hope and assurance, an inner knowledge of her at-one-ness with God and with all creation. She has written this book to encourage her readers to be still and to allow themselves to be led through the layers of their own consciousness to that same knowledge.

This is a book to be pondered, reflected upon, read with the heart, so that we can come to know for ourselves this God, so real yet so elusive, so frightening yet so attractive.

The spirituality this book presents is earthed in the reality of human experience of pain. The author knows depression and despair, yet writes: "When we, in our deepest despair, spiral ever downwards, and go towards the numbness of nothing, we are actually travelling upwards towards our Christ" (ch. 4, p. 89).

The book is free of the gloomy predictions, warnings and woes so beloved of some who are called visionaries, and presents a most attractive God, a God who laughs, who, while sharing our sufferings on the Cross, says, "Give them honey" (ch. 4, p. 85), who delights in romantic love, for whom the gods and goddesses of paganism are not demonic enemies to be rejected, but are part of God's plan.

Read this book slowly, read it with your heart, and you will begin to hear the music of it in your own bruised heart, and you will know with an inner assurance the truth of the final sentence of the last chapter: "The future is totally blessed for all generations to come."

*G. W. H.*
*Australia, March 1994*

# Prologue

When it was suggested that I should write a book of my spiritual experiences, I knew that I would like to try, but the task seemed too daunting, the sheer physical effort of putting all that I am into words seemed too much. At that time, I was occupied in making copies of my prayer picture tapes. These, which were widely circulated to convents and to people in adversity, drew many favourable comments.

By this time, although brought up as a nominal Anglican, I felt that my spiritual home was in Rome. As I was unable to travel, I asked my husband Mark to make a pilgrimage to the Vatican on my behalf. He went in November 1991, taking with him two batches of tapes; one for His Holiness Pope John-Paul II; the other for Fr Peter-Hans Kolvenbach, the Superior General of the Society of Jesus. The reaction from both was heartening; the latter in particular suggesting that I should help others by sharing my spiritual experience. This was the spur I needed.

I received a great deal of support and encouragement from other quarters, notably Fr John Coventry SJ and Fr Gerard Hughes SJ, and of course from my dear Sisters in various convents. It seemed that the time was at last right, and after much planning, I began laboriously to dictate into my tape recorder in May 1992.

The following months were fraught. Extreme fatigue, a succession of infections and viruses, and having to relive again the more traumatic parts of my life, made progress difficult. It did not help when the right words simply would not come; when I was unable to portray my feelings vividly enough, and more than once frustration made me want to abandon the whole thing and destroy what had been done. But then, talking to my dear friends, I found that I must press on. The same words were repeated endlessly over the telephone, "You must complete it. You simply must complete it!" And so, heartened and encouraged, I continued. Here it is.

Many books on Christian faith are cerebral. They assume that the reader has an intimate knowledge of the Bible, and make great demands on the intellect. Others are commentaries on the lives of saints, or the writings of medieval mystics such as Julian of Norwich; Meister Eckhart, or Hildegard of Bingen, to name but a few. The impression they give is that it is difficult to make spiritual progress unless one is either possessed of great learning, or has spent one's life within a religious order.

By contrast, mine is a simple story. I was born into a poor family in North London, and the Church played little part in my life until my later years. Due to ill-health, I received virtually no schooling. Only long afterwards did I realize that this was actually to my advantage; that my untutored mind was an ideal fallow field for my Lord to sow, and later to harvest. My life has been perhaps harder than the normal, but I have learned to endure what cannot be altered, with only my own inner strength to sustain me. Endurance, coupled with love and faith have been the keynotes of my life, and through them I have been blessed beyond all measure.

At first I considered relating only my spiritual experiences, but the story would then have been incomplete. I wanted to show that Christian contemplation is within the reach of anyone who has faith and perseverance. It is not the exclusive preserve of the intellectual, the highly educated, the naturally saintly, or the full-time religious. It is for everyone who wants it badly enough. The path is not easy, but it is there, straight and true.

As I write, the fields are being harvested. For me it is a double celebration; the completion of what for me has been a mammoth task, but which gives me a great sense of achievement, and the Harvest Festival. I especially love Harvest Festival. It is a homely time; a time that I can enjoy and share with the world; a time when families gather joyfully together to celebrate the bounty of the Earth.

In many ways, finishing this book at harvest time is symbolic. Like the old year, I am in the autumn of my life, and rather to my surprise, have found it rich and fulfilling, which I had not expected. My family and friends have given me such loving support, and enabled me to live a full life. Our Lord who died on the cross for us has shown me that the two greatest powers in heaven and earth are love and suffering. We each have our own chalices that we fill with a vintage grown, harvested and pressed during our lives, and at the end, one drinks one's own vintage and one's own sacrament, for this is the life you have lived. Lift your chalice to your lips and drink deeply from it.

# CHAPTER 1

# The sowing and growing time

I was an unpromising seed in the Lord's garden. The youngest of five children, I was born with a strange veinous condition in my right leg, stretching from hip to toes, which made it look like a hideous tree trunk grafted onto a baby's body. Whenever I put my weight on it, it hurt. My earliest memories are of having to favour my bad leg whenever I stood or walked, even as a toddler.

My mother was a tower of strength to me throughout her entire life. It must have been so very hard for her to have to watch me limp around, knowing that the doctors had said that I could not be expected to live past ten years old. It must have been even harder for her to take me to endless hospitals, where the doctors merely hoped that they might be able to do something to help. And twice in my young life, she was forced to sit helplessly at my bedside while I hovered between this world and the next. But if she shed tears, I was never allowed to see them.

My stays in hospital usually lasted several weeks; time enough to grow used to life in the ward. In those days, the 1930s, hospital visitors were actively discouraged, so I saw

Mum but rarely. The nurses became my family at these times. I cried when I had to leave home to go into hospital, but I also cried when the time came to leave the calm and orderly surroundings of the ward to return to my noisy and crowded home. Fortunately children adapt very quickly. I learned that lesson very early in life, a lesson which helped sustain me through the very difficult times to come.

Most of my early memories of hospital have long since been washed away by torrents of tears, but at quite a young age, I learned to hear the voice. It was a grown-up voice. When I was in pain, or upset, it would say to me:

"Be still. All is well. Be still and quiet now. I am with you. This time will end. This time will pass."

I learned to prick up my inner ears and listen to this familiar voice, and sure enough, peace was soon restored to me. The voice also showed me how to step into another world and leave the bars of the big hospital cot behind, to enter the world of my imagination. In this other world I was out and about, perhaps in the woods among the bluebells, mingling with fairies and elves. They became my magic companions, and were as real to me as the people who walked around the ward. There were two Dorothys. One lived at home, or in the ward; the other dwelt in her own secret world, a world where there were no partings, no nagging pains, no terrible handicaps to overcome, and all was happiness and joy.

When I was at home I was convalescent for much of the time, but whenever I felt well enough I played in the street with children of my own age. I was adventurous, and loved to climb, even though a fall might have been disastrous. I defied this leg of mine that hurt so much. I wanted to be as other children, and do all the things that they did, even though I did limp heavily.

I was no Pollyanna. I was a spirited child, even imperious at times, and not easily put upon. When thwarted I often gave way to temper tantrums, lying flat on my back on the floor, kicking the door with my good foot, while screaming at the top of my voice. These outbursts were usually rewarded with a hearty slap on the top of my good leg!

My early years were packed with incident. I should like to tell you about them, but that would need a book of its own. Perhaps one day I shall write it. We were a poor family, living in a council house in North London. Poverty meant little at that time, as everyone around us was in the same straits. People helped each other through the difficulties and hardships of life in those days, and our spirit was always cheerful. Even when the Blitz started, and we cowered beneath the kitchen table as the German bombs rained down and the house shook from the explosions, we were not downhearted.

Most of my friends were evacuated to the country during the Blitz, but I strongly resisted the idea. Not until the late Spring of 1941, when the bombing had all but ended, was it forced upon me, when I was sent to a special home for frail and handicapped children. There I saw the English countryside for the first time, and real cows. My two years there were basically happy, but I was often in hot water through being quick to react against what I saw as injustice. At one point I even tried to run away, with the idea of walking back to London! Fortunately, my attempt was an ignominious failure. Finally Mum brought me home.

15

Hardly had I arrived home when I was stricken with appendicitis, and was rushed to hospital for emergency surgery. This turned into full-blown peritonitis, which I barely survived. For weeks I hovered on the brink of the next world, and was only pulled back by an event which in retrospect seems miraculous. My recovery lasted seven months. At last I returned home, but not for long. Although barely convalescent, I borrowed my uncle's bicycle on the sly, and fell and broke my bad leg, ending up back in the same hospital, in plaster from armpits to ankle. And if this wasn't enough, the hospital was badly bombed, with many casualties. I was evacuated to Halifax in Yorkshire on a hospital train. When after several months the plaster was removed, I was able to walk only with the aid of crutches.

These were disastrous times, but my inner voice was always there to comfort me, even if it did not always speak to me in so many words. Faith, though, has always played a great part in my life; faith and an inner certainty. But my faith did not come through orthodox religion; that came to me very late in life.

Although nominally Anglican, my family were not church-goers. My first encounter with organized religion came when I started Sunday School when I was about seven. I could not attend every Sunday, my health did not permit, but I enjoyed singing hymns, and saying simple prayers with the other children. I was not strong enough to attend school, but my sister Bobbie had taught me to read. Sometimes I tried to read the Bible, but the language was strange to me; I couldn't really understand it.

I had one close friend, whose family was very religious.

16

They had large framed texts on the walls: God Is Love, or The Good Shepherd Is Always Watching Us. I read them, but they didn't mean anything to me. Her sisters were very solemn and didn't seem to have any play in them, unlike my sisters, who spent most of their time singing, dancing or fighting.

I gradually came to realize that most people saw only the shadow of God and Jesus. They saw an image that to me seemed sterile, prim and proper. They acted as though He only visited us on Sundays, when we were on our best behaviour, and never really got to know us at all. But instinctively I knew better.

I began to plague Mum with questions about God. Did God like this, and does He know about something else; questions that were very important to me. Mum, far more concerned with Dad's likes and dislikes for dinner than with the preferences of the Supreme Being, brushed my questions aside as being of no consequence.

My other encounter with organized religion was equally disappointing. Not far away there stood a community hall outside which was a poster proclaiming "Everyone Welcome. Come and be Healed". Dad, who was out of work at that time, decided to take me, hoping against hope for a miracle.

It was a poor little place, with plain wooden chairs and a makeshift altar. After a short service, the healing started. Then it was my turn. The minister and his helpers solemnly gathered around me, hands clasped piously together, and said a prayer, asking that this little child be healed. I sat perfectly still and waited. I waited for a roll of thunder, possibly accompanied by a flash of lightning, to announce

17

my instantaneous cure.

Nothing happened. I felt let down; I felt I had let the others down somehow by not being cured. The service drew to a close, and we left. It was all strangely unreal; a feeling of "What was that all about?". The notice outside almost amounted to a guarantee, but the promise had not been fulfilled.

\*    \*    \*    \*    \*

The war ended shortly after my return from Halifax. I managed to attend school for four months in what was my final year, but was so far behind my contemporaries that it was of little value. My lack of education meant that the only jobs open to me were in factories, but I was too frail for these. My transition from girl to woman was difficult. As far as I was able, I joined in the activities of my peers, but the things I could not do caused much heartache. Buying shoes was always a sad time; I had to buy sensible, granny shoes when I really wanted smart high heels. Clothes were another problem; I was tall and slim, but my crutches pulled at whatever I wore and they never looked quite right.

I had to learn to overcome envy, and not to lose my self-esteem, which is difficult when one is young. I was always terribly aware of my lack of schooling, and rather in awe of people who seemed educated. At dances, skating rinks and swimming pools, I was always the one left at the table, always the onlooker. Often my spirit flew around the ice rink as my physical self sat watching. Watching with a deep sadness that never in this world could I do these things.

18

I always tried to be cheerful, and never let anyone see what was going on inside me. I must have succeeded, because crutches, bad leg or no, I had as many boy friends as my peers, and seemed to be popular with them. In turn I enjoyed their company.

I had always enjoyed life, but as I neared maturity it became enhanced even more. I felt a life force, an energy, entering me strongly. I started to take immense pleasure in being different from my friends, and in questioning them. They seemed to have little feeling for things. Sometimes I would ask them if they found the earth very beautiful; the sky, the sun, the flowers and the trees. They would simply say something like "Here she goes again" and try to brush me off.

To me, this was the religious experience of life. Dad died at about this time, and of course I attended his funeral, but the service didn't seem to mean much. Going to church had little to offer. It was boring compared to the everyday living I was experiencing. Neither vicars nor sermons gave me the food I craved. They just spoke to me of times past; of the historical Lord and of biblical teachings. They said nothing about this tremendously exhilarating life force which I was tapping into. I felt no need of church, because it seemed that I carried my own Christ-talk with me. It belonged to life; I was living it as I was meant to. By comparison, church seemed dead; devoid of juice.

I became increasingly frustrated at having to use crutches. By my twentieth birthday it had become an obsession. I wanted to walk on my two feet; I wanted to be able to carry my own shopping bags. Even my handbag had to be carried on my shoulder with a long strap. Finally it was too

19

much. I asked for an appointment with an orthopaedic surgeon.

He told me that he could fix my knee to make it permanently straight, but it would be stronger, and that I would be able to walk without crutches. He also warned that the operation would be extremely dangerous. I wanted to walk properly so much that I barely hesitated.

I needed a massive blood transfusion during the operation because I was haemorrhaging badly all the time, but finally it was over and I was taken back to the ward. It was now that the surgeon's worst fears were realized. The veins burst open, but because my leg was encased in plaster, this was not readily apparent; nor could anything be done before the plaster was removed. Post-operative shock was compounded by infection. In the days that followed, the pain between the morphia injections was excruciating. My family gathered around, but they had become shadowy. Once more the angel of death hovered, waiting. A little girl inside me knew him of old. He was familiar, and not at all to be feared. I was gladly slipping into his warm arms. He was my Lord, he was so close, unbelievably close. I welcomed Him, I wanted to go; to be done with it.

The fever subsided, but I had lost the will to live. I could not eat; would not eat. I looked at myself in a hand mirror. My face was gaunt, yellow skin stretched tightly over a skull, with huge, glistening beads of sweat. My life hung by the slimmest thread, about to snap. The nurses were gentle and soothing, but luckily the ward sister knew better. She stood at the foot of my bed and shouted at me.

"If you don't eat, you're going to be on the mortuary slab

20

tonight. Eat or you're dead, my girl!"

Being shouted at gave me the most enormous jolt. I wasn't used to anger. I asked for a fried egg sandwich, of all the ridiculous things. It was rubbery and horrid, but I ate it. I started to recover.

A further thirteen operations followed, at weekly intervals, mainly to have the steel rods in my knee tightened to push the edges of the bones together. This wasn't so good, but I endured it, as I had endured so much else. Then after six months in bed, I was at last allowed up. Although my leg was now delightfully straight, it was much shorter than the other, and I needed an orthopaedic shoe. This was duly made, and for the first time in years my foot touched the ground. Slowly I progressed, from crutches to two sticks, then finally to one stick. Shortly after my twenty-first birthday, I was allowed home. At last I could do all the things others took for granted, such as carrying a cup across a room, or a bag out of a shop. I had earned them.

As I grew stronger, I became restless. I wanted to earn my keep; to have a measure of independence like my friends. I was still not strong enough for factory work, but with my lack of schooling what else could I do? In the end I was sent to a rehabilitation centre in Surrey, where my natural aptitudes could be assessed. To my delight I, who had always loved talking to people, had an aptitude for telephone work. I was then sent on a Post Office course in South Kensington, and trained as a telephonist. Like most of my friends, I now had an office job. It seemed too good to be true.

One by one, my friends married. I was joyful for them, but I could never imagine getting married myself, even

21

though a young American called Don had proposed to me two years earlier. Then one evening, our eyes met across a crowded room. His name was Mark, and we made a date for the following evening. After a turbulent courtship, we married just nine months later.

We were two strong-minded people, with very decided opinions on everything. Often these were conflicting, and we argued and fought, loved and made up, continually. Our early life together was loving, passionate, sometimes stormy, but never dull. Only one thing was missing. I wanted a child quite desperately.

The gynaecologist I consulted advised against it. I could not have a normal delivery; it would have to be a Caesarian, and for me, this would be extremely dangerous. It could cost my life. I determined to take the risk. I had exceptional reasons for doing so. I had never tasted the full richness of life. I had never been able to run, to dance, to walk barefoot across sand, nor even walk at all without limping heavily. Now with all my heart, I wanted to create a healthy child, that would grow up and do all the things I had been unable to do. It was my dearest wish.

Pregnant at last, I was once again forced to take to my bed, where I grew rounder and rounder like a pumpkin. At last the day arrived, and I was admitted to hospital once again. For once there were no problems, and a few weeks later I was proudly pushing my shiny new pram, with my beautiful new baby in it. My happiness was complete, and I blessed the day when I had had the operation on my knee, for I could pick my little one up and walk with her in my arms, just like any mum in all the world. I had done it!

More years passed, my baby turned into an exhausting

toddling tornado, then into a little girl who held my hand as she skipped alongside me. We bought our first car, which gave me greater freedom than I had ever before known, and moved from London to the country. Life was perfect. There was but one cloud on the horizon. My new friends were all young mothers, and their conversation consisted of little more than new clothes, teething and nappy rash. I tried to draw them out, with callow questions like: "What is the meaning of the universe?"

Their eyes immediately glazed over, and they mumbled that they had never really thought about it, adding that the corner shop had some cheap plums. I learned not to ask such questions. There was only one time during this period when God allowed me to expand myself mentally and spiritually. Colin Urquhart was a young curate assigned to our parish. He had many thoughts that were food for my starving soul, and often he would find his way to my kitchen, where over coffee and biscuits we would explore the deeper meanings of life, of Christianity, and of the universe. But all too soon he was moved on, much to my sorrow.

My daughter grew, and from frilly dresses and dancing classes progressed to jodphurs and riding lessons. All her activities were sheer delight to me, even when one day she came home in a smelly state and announced that she and her friends had been riding a pig. But these idyllic years were not to last. My body, weakened by years of ill health and disability, once more started to betray me. The spirit was so willing, but now I had to endure the weakness of the flesh. I could do less and less housework before the pain worsened, and I had to rest more and more. I learned to

23

pace myself, but still sometimes I overdid things and became exhausted.

We moved yet again, to a small market town in the Fens. My daughter left school and started work; she was growing up fast. I could still get out in the car, and often we stopped in quiet country lanes to give me a run in my wheelchair, out in the fresh air among the trees and hedgerows. Several years passed like this; then came a terrible sadness. Mum, by now nearing eighty, died.

I took her death very badly. She had been with me all through my traumatic childhood; the rock on which I leaned. Now she was gone. So deep was my grief that I no longer wanted to live. As always in times of trouble, I turned to our Lord. I prayed, and my prayers were answered in a strange and wonderful way. I began to dream; vivid dreams in which I met Mum again. I met her often, and we talked. She seemed to be in much happier surroundings, and looked younger than I remembered. With this, my grief eased, for I knew she was with me. Even waking I could feel her presence. But it took many years to get over my loss, and learn to live without her.

Meanwhile my right leg became less and less able to bear my weight, and I had increasing difficulty in breathing. A cardiac specialist came home to see me. His prognosis was not good. The ordeals that I had endured from birth had taken their toll. My heart and lungs were very tired from the constant exertion needed to do even such a simple thing as walking, and I must now rest almost all the time.

When this first happened, and I knew beyond a shadow of a doubt that I must stay indoors all the time, the years ahead stretched interminably; years without end it seemed.

I ached dreadfully for the outdoors; anywhere outside the house, but this was denied me. I became an indoor person, pallid, shut away from the sun. My friends came to see me, ruddy and tanned, fresh from the seaside or holiday. They could go out at will, for a whole day or for just five minutes as the mood took them. These things were now forbidden me. My home now became a place of confinement. Sometimes it seemed that my front door had bars on it; it was a prison door that kept me from the outside world.

It was heartbreaking. I felt totally and utterly useless. I was a normal person trapped within a failing body, and I had great difficulty in coming to terms with it. I entered a deep depression; there no longer seemed any point in going on. The years ahead looked bleak and barren. All these years my family had been restricted in their activities because of me, and I had suffered guilt and anger in consequence. And now things were to be even worse. My old spirit deserted me, and I felt completely worthless; worse than a failure. I was a nothing.

I could just manage to walk from one room to another, but I was unable to sit up for more than a few minutes at a time. I was most comfortable lying completely flat, with a cushion beneath my head. Fortunately my couch was long enough to allow this. At least I had somewhere to rest apart from bed. The days were long, and were to always be so from this moment, for there was little to distract me. Little to help the hands of the clock fly round, as they do if one is engaged in housework, or some other task.

Learning to accept this was not easy. First came a hard and difficult period when I rebelled; I kicked against it. The busy housewife that I once had been had long since learned to be still, for it had been many years since I had been able to cook, or polish the furniture, or do any of the myriad chores that are a housewife's daily lot. Now I had an even more bitter lesson to learn.

Sometimes I would for one fleeting moment forget that I could no longer go out, only to feel an inner wrench at having once more to face the inevitable. Frustration and tears followed. Many, many tears. Tears of rage at the unfairness of life. It was hard to cope, but I had to learn; the whole family had to learn, and adjust. In time I was to find a doorway, through which lay immeasurable pleasures. But I had not yet found this door, nor did I even suspect its existence.

The nearest I could now get to the outside world was by looking through the patio doors into the garden. Mine is only a small garden, but very private and enclosed, with a tall hedge at the bottom, and high fences to the sides. It is packed with plants and shrubs, and filled with gloriously coloured flowers and foliage for most of the year. And of course my birds. I have many varieties of bird in my garden.

As the years passed, my garden gave me a new perception of time. It was a clock of a different sort; a slower but much more satisfying clock, which showed time by seasons rather than hours. This came to mean more to me now, in this new phase of my life.

Winter was both a sorrowing time and a waiting time; sorrowing for past glories, and waiting for the new glories to come. Spring was the season of renewal, of saying hello again to the dear friends of the previous year as their tender green shoots burst into life. Summer meant fullness and abundance; a time of ripening, of gathering and harvesting, followed by Autumn, the season of falling leaves and mists, the time of clearing away the old to make room for the new.

With this new, slow-paced life, I had time to drift back; all the time in the world; time to see how my life reflected the seasonal changes. This I could see, life itself unfolding. I had been given a blessing, to learn about time. Seasonal, biological, natural time. Even eternal time! Behind doors, mysterious and shrouded at first, lay strange places that one day I would enter. This was my escape from everlasting gazing at the ceiling or the walls of my room. An escape back into times remembered; times of bright colours; of once familiar places, and precious activity.

This was no idle daydreaming; it was given me for a purpose. Looking back, I see what I was, and what I have become. Long ago I learned that yearning for what I could not have is destructive. It sows the seeds of bitterness, and carries unhappiness in its wake. One thing that I did have in abundance was time. The real enemy is not time; it is boredom. It is boredom that makes five minutes seem an hour; boredom that slows the hands of the clock. Some people actually said that they envied me in having so much time, but when I asked them if they would be willing to swap lives, they shied away. For a little while perhaps, but not for a lifetime. Only one said that she would. A devout Christian, she wanted peace and quiet to find God. She thought that my life had given me a tremendous opportunity. She was right of course, but I couldn't see it at the time. God was calling me, but I couldn't yet hear His voice distinctly. But looking back, I was greatly blessed;

27

although denied the activity of the body, I was given activity of the spirit.

Gradually I found a new role; that of helping others. People began to turn to me with their troubles; my friends, then their friends, who quickly became my friends also. They would often telephone, or call to see me. Active people were too busy with their own affairs to have the time or interest for others, but I, at home for twenty-four hours a day with little to do, was easily accessible. Without at first realizing it, I became an anchoress, and my home was my cell.

My life so far had been a growing time. I had endured the frosts, the storms, and the droughts. Now the ripening time was at hand, to be followed by a harvest beyond my wildest dreams.

# CHAPTER 2

# The ripening

There are two sorts of dreams. Some are ordinary, while others are special. I always knew when my dreams were special. In ordinary dreams, the colours were normal, and when I moved, I always limped heavily. In special dreams, colours were brighter, everything was crystal clear, and I walked and ran effortlesly. Now I was given an extraordinarily vivid dream.

I was standing in a cemetery at the foot of a grave. Looking at the headstone, I saw my own name carved there. I saw the dates of birth and death, but these had no real significance for me, and I felt quite calm. As I watched, the headstone slowly grew, and changed into a wooden door. I drifted towards it, and unseen hands opened it for me.

Passing through, I found to my amazement that I had entered a small country church, of which my door was a side door. It was peaceful, but deserted. The highly polished pews shone, and black and white marble floor tiles led to a simple carved wooden altar, covered in a white cloth, in the centre of which was a crucifix. I stood there for a moment in the silence, feeling the presence of a calm and loving spirit. Almost it seemed that I could hear songs of praise sung in ages past, echoing oh so faintly from the walls.

Opposite the door by which I had entered was the main door of the church. I passed through it, to find myself standing on rich green grass. A voice spoke.

"Walk to the end of the field."

I did so and, from nowhere, a hill appeared. This did not seem at all surprising to me, that a hill should thus suddenly appear. Again the voice spoke.

"Look up upon the hill."

I looked up, and was at once humbled, for there at the summit was the most enormous cross, of plain wood, hewn from some gigantic tree. I gazed up at it as it towered above me, my neck arched hard back in order to see the top. It seemed alive, and radiated immense, solid strength, as if to say, I am above all humanity, yet of it. I stood there in wonder, mixed with reverence for all that it portrayed through the ages. For thousands of years it seemed to have stood there.

And then, to my horror, orange flames started licking from its base where it met the bright green grass. I grew frightened and darted forward to beat them out with my hands, but to my surprise they did not burn me. The flames were cool. The voice spoke again.

"All is well. You will see."

The flames spread steadily up the cross as though to consume it, and as they went they changed colour. Every individual flame was different; pink, blue, yellow, violet, all the colours of the rainbow, and others never seen upon

30

this earth. They shone with a clear crystal light, caressing and enveloping the whole of this monumental cross with such loving gentleness, and such beauty, that I fell on my knees before it and feared it, for I had seen the spirit of the wood of the cross. Our Lord Jesus had shown himself to me in the very colours of before time began, muted for my mortal eyes to see. I awoke from this dream full of reverence.

*     *     *     *     *

I commenced a quest to find my Lord. Not the God to be found in books, or in any form of learning, but the spirit within. I sought him through prayer, deep and intense prayer. My routine was always the same. After breakfast, I returned to bed, knowing that I would not be disturbed. I tried to open myself fully to Him. Time and again I said to Him,

"Do what You wish with me my Lord. Do what You will. My life is Yours. Show me the way." I became utterly a servant to him.

Constant pain makes one tense, and I began to realize that in deep meditative prayer, I was relaxing my body; smoothing away the tensions. I learned to relax completely, even in broad daylight. The awareness of light, of noises from the outside world; even of pain itself, faded to nothing as my senses went deeper and deeper into the meditative state.

Unknowingly, in my most fervent attempts to find my Lord, I had gone beyond meditation, into deep contemplative prayer. I had entered an interior awareness of prayer so deep that it became an entrance to my own living spirit. The door had opened for me.

It was now that I encountered Hashamhet. At first I heard only his voice. It was a familiar voice; a voice such as I had known in childhood. He told me his name; that he was a teacher, and that he had been sent to me. He said that many things were going to be shown me, and that many other teachers would come.

Later I was allowed to see an image of him. He was youngish, perhaps in his thirties. He was clean shaven, with dark, almost black hair, with what looked like ringlets down both sides of his face. He wore a black hat with a sharp brim, and a long black frock coat buttoned down the front, reaching to the floor. He told me that he was a rabbi.

A rabbi? I was completely bewildered. I had been questing for my Lord Jesus and a rabbi had appeared? Where had I gone wrong? Was it all a figment of my imagination? My mind in turmoil, I did the only thing I could think of. I prayed for guidance, but all I received in answer was a compulsion to follow the path that had led me this far. But soon I was to be overtaken by even stranger events.

It was the morning of January 6, 1986; Epiphany, although I didn't know it at the time. I was lying in my bed in a state of deepest contemplation, unaware of external light or noise. Gradually a picture started to form. At first it was vague, rather fuzzy and out of focus, with a sort of dreamlike quality. The scene was a village in the Middle East. Many people were walking around, wearing long flowing robes and loose headdresses.

"You are going to the Land of Smiles. No frowns are

allowed there."

It was of course Hashamhet. As he spoke, the scene became clearer, and I seemed to enter the picture. I saw many people, mainly women but some men, all chattering and laughing around me. It was very hot, and the sun shone brilliantly. I experienced the feeling of an, oh, such a happy land.

A young woman, barely more than a girl, came forward from the throng. Her eyes were dark brown, shining with laughter, and her skin was brown also, pulsing with youth and vitality, against which her even white teeth flashed in startling contrast. I could see a little of her hair, which was black and glossy. Her robe was a dark dusty red; her headcloth was apricot with a dark red border, crisscrossed with a trellis pattern in the same colour.

She smiled at me, a smile made even more attractive by the fact that her headcloth had slipped askew, forcing her to look at me slightly sideways. This made the girl/ woman impression even stronger. I felt that she had been a mischievous child, and that her emergence into womanhood had been too recent to have entirely erased the girl. Yet at the same time I saw maturity and wisdom, which sat strangely but happily at odds with the youthfulness of her lovely face.

Turning, she set off through the village at a run, moving as gracefully as a young gazelle, the while beckoning me to follow. A gold bracelet gleamed on her slim brown arm as she urged me on. I followed her. I did not run, but somehow just followed, keeping pace easily as she led me down narrow pathways between the buildings, all the while urging me on with that radiant smile, and beckoning to me, on, on, follow me.

It was so very hot, and the sunlight was incredibly bright, although the buildings cast deep shadows, giving some relief as we sped through the byways of that biblical village. At last we arrived at a plain wrought iron gate, set in an archway in a stone wall. It was not locked. She opened it and passed through. I followed, leaving the gate open behind me.

I found myself in a stone-paved courtyard, in the full glare of the blinding sun. At first I could see little; the colours were bleached out by the brilliant light, but as my eyes became accustomed to the glare, I began to make out details.

The courtyard was enclosed by white stone walls, in which green plants with great fronds were growing, giving the impression of a cool green mist through the shimmering heat. On my left was a rectangular pool, with shadowy shapes of fishes barely visible deep beneath the surface. Nearby was a small fountain, bubbling and gurgling gently. Unbidden, I bent right down and put my hands in it, feeling the wonderful coolness and freshness of the living water, which contrasted so greatly with the tremendous heat and brilliance of the sun. The young woman was standing a few paces away, smiling down at me. I asked her name.

"It is Ayesha," she told me, and once again I was struck by her dark eyes, so bright with laughter. Turning, she led the way across the courtyard towards the house. It was a long, low building, not opulent but substantial, with a verandah running its entire length, the sort of house in which a well-to-do merchant might live.

Three steps led up to the verandah, and mounting them, I noticed that the entire wall was composed of open arches. Inside it was cool and shady, and blinded by the glare from outside, at first I could see little. But as my eyes adjusted to the shade, I saw that it was a hall rather than a room, the far wall of which had arches like the side by which I had entered. Through them lay another courtyard like the first with patches of green vegetation rippling in the heat haze.

The floor beneath my feet was of cool wooden boards, dark and smooth from years of loving polishing, their patina gleaming softly. Richly patterned rugs were scattered around, their colours mainly cream, apricot, and that lovely browny red which I had first noticed in Ayesha's robe, and cream fringes contrasting happily with the dark polished floor.

There were many low couches; covered in a cream-coloured woven material, and on them were very large cushions, of a silky appearance and with the same colour theme as the rugs; dark red-brown, apricot and cream. I heard music playing softly; where it came from I did not know, but it was not Eastern. It was the love theme from Tchaikovsky's Romeo and Juliet Fantasy Overture. It was just there in the background, filling the air with peace and happiness.

Meanwhile Ayesha was flittering around the hall, smoothing cushions and rearranging things. She moved swiftly and delicately, all the while giving me laughing sideways glances. Her headcloth had slipped even further, and now I could see that her shiny black hair was pulled back, framing her lovely young brown face, so full of life and laughter and love. Her gestures said feel welcome, be welcome, be at home.

I sat down on one of the couches. It was very low, and I arranged myself sideways with my ankles crossed. It was such a comfortable position in which to sit, and one that ordinarily is denied me. I noticed now that I was wearing a long cream coloured robe, for my legs were covered by it.

Looking around me, I saw that there were low tables here and there, with ornate gilded legs, some with golden jugs on their shiny surfaces. There was no food that I could see, nor even drinking goblets; just the jugs. Outside the sun beat down, and the greenery stirred slightly in a gentle breeze. I sat there in the coolness and shade, and relaxed.

More young girls entered and joined Ayesha, all chattering and laughing and moving around. They seemed glad to have me there with them, and we delighted in each other's company. This was such a lovely, such a happy place to be, and I was made to feel so welcome; so at home.

A man entered the room; a solid man, with a deep chest and broad shoulders covered by his oatmeal-coloured robe. Ayesha brought him over to me. His skin was paler than hers. He was well into his middle years, and he had a very white beard, setting off rosy, rounded cheeks. He smiled and laughed, and his blue eyes crinkled at me with delight.

He had an air of strength and responsibility; this was a man to lean on. Without conscious thought, I rose and went to him. His arms opened in welcome, and he held me close, like a long-lost daughter, his eyes twinkling down at me in pure joy. I thought that I would smile and laugh back at him, but no; I started crying against his chest. Not tears of sadness, but of utter overwhelming relief.

36

"Here you belong," he told me gently. "Here you are wanted, very much wanted."

I had so longed for this welcome; I had so much joy at this homecoming that I must weep, and with my tears wash away those very long and lonely years when I felt that I was a nuisance to those around me, and not really wanted by anybody. Here, in the strong arms of this big man, I was at last wanted. Ayesha smiled at me, and the words formed in my mind, "Yes, you are home." I asked his name, and he told me that it was Absolom. I truly felt that I had come home at last. Ayesha handed Absolom a piece of soft cloth with which to wipe away my tears.

At this point I left the picture, and rose back through the layers of consciousness, like a diver returning from the deep. Back in my bed, I reached for a tissue, for tears were streaming uncontrollably down my face. But it was not my hand that wiped them away; it was a much stronger hand than mine, with the touch of a loving father, firmly, as if to say, "Enough tears now, enough. Let them begone now; you are home." And so it was; I was whole, I was home.

Afterwards I asked myself, had this been some sort of magic carpet ride? What had happened? It had been like a story from the Arabian Nights. But for whom? To tell to whom? I knew not. Yet in the middle of these tumultuous thoughts, I was aware of such gladness of heart that I could not describe just how good I felt. I had come alive, beautifully and vibrantly alive. Once again I had seen colours that were not of this world, in a perfectly formed picture that I had entered, in which I had felt the warmth of the sun; a picture in which I had walked. Oddly, it was not strange to me, and yet I was amazed by it. Like Alice,

I had gone down a rabbit hole and entered another world, a world more real to me than the world to which I had returned.

The wonder of this experience was such that I felt impelled to record it. My radio cassette recorder was always on my bed, and I reached for a tape. Alas, it was an old and much used one, sad and scratchy, but it would serve. Closing my eyes, I lay back and faithfully recorded my adventure.

*     *     *     *     *

The pattern of my life was unchanging. Next morning after breakfast, once more I entered a deep contemplative state. Down through the layers of awareness I went, peeling them back one by one like the skins of an onion, leaving the world behind, until at last my eyelids grew dark. To my surprise another picture started to form. At first I could not believe it. Had it been my own fancy yesterday? Was I asking for it again today? I tried to shut it out. I was unable to do so. I was told,

"Rest and let it be. Let it be!"

I relaxed, and the picture started building up. Once more I was to walk into the picture. To my unbelieving delight and joy, this became the pattern of the days that followed. At first I received a new picture every day, then after a while they became intermittent. Of course, I never knew which might be the last, but was always prepared for them to cease. I was grateful for those I had had, and each was faithfully recorded. Why, I did not know; I only knew that I must.

Each picture was different; no two were ever the same. Over and over I was told that all was not what it seemed, that there was a deeper meaning. Look for the word in the picture. It is a conundrum, solve the riddle, and sure enough, each seemed to have a lesson in it, although I was often a long while in discovering it. I was also puzzled by my growing collection of tapes, and I often asked my Lord,

"What do I do with them? Who are they for?"

"All will be shown to you in time. All will become clear". But patience had never been a virtue of mine, and I had to learn to be patient and wait, to wait for His time, not mine. All the early pictures had Middle Eastern settings, and dark skinned people. Many of them seemed to promise journeys, but there was never a departure. At last my impatience spilled over, and I asked why. My question was answered by another picture.

In this, I started in a high place, looking down over a great city. The houses and buildings were white, with graceful colonnades, Ancient Greek in appearance. Half the city was bathed in brilliant sunshine, but the half I was standing above was in shadow, cast by a mountain on my left that I sensed rather than saw. The sky was the most gorgeous blue.

I stood there, gazing down, for what seemed a long time. After a while, the city began to descend, until I could see only blue sky, with rooftops far below. And then, to my incredulous delight, there came a magical white horse. He had enormous wings on his back, smaller ones on his rear hooves, and he galloped and flew, frolicked and pranced around me, his head tossing and his mane flying in the wind.

I stood like a child, rapt in wonderment at this spectacle of a flying horse, so enormously strong and full of life, as he turned and thundered towards me. As he came to a halt, he reared high above me, showing his creamy underbelly, broad and strong, then came down on all four hooves, and stood quietly just in front of me. Moving closer, I reached out and stroked his sleek flanks and smooth neck. He rolled his eyes at me, showing the whites, and I knew that he was only part tamed.

Leaning forward, I put my face against him. He was ready to be off; I could feel the nervous energy quivering within him. I laughed a little, and said "Shall I ride you?" I was not seriously thinking of doing it, but then I found myself on his back. I felt then that I had entered some fairy story or legend, for I became part of him. For an instant I saw myself through other eyes. I had very golden hair, cut short in bobble curls, and wore a short tunic. My feet and legs were bare. Wrapping his mane firmly around my fingers, I gripped his sides with my knees, and we were off!

The sheer exaltation of flying through the air on this magnificent beast was beyond all description. On and on we went, through the blue sky, passing small fluffy clouds to left and right. We journeyed seemingly endlessly. I asked the horse's name, and was shown it written in Greek characters. I could not read it, and so said, "I shall call you Pegasus."

At last another land appeared in the distance; another city. As we drew nearer I could see greenery, and white buildings with golden spires. In my mind I heard a name that sounded like "Athlon," and knew then that I was indeed in a Greek legend; a place of myths and ancient gods.

40

We swung high over the city. Below, I saw squares of neatly cut, beautifully kept lawns, while the streets were lined with wonderful buildings of white marble, with colonnades and plinths with gilded edges, all shining brightly in the sun. Slowly we descended, and landed gently on a beautifully manicured lawn. I slid off Pegasus. The grass felt extraordinary under my bare feet, soft to walk upon, like a luxurious carpet. Not only the buildings, but the paths were of smooth white marble, with that wonderful smooth feel that only marble has.

Suddenly I heard voices. I turned, and saw a magnificent building, a veritable palace, that outshone all the rest in grandeur. It was Palladian in style, with tall colonnades and a pitched roof. Down the many steps leading from it tumbled a crowd of people, laughing as they came. They were dressed in robes of all the delicate colours of sweet peas; pinks and blues, peaches and lavenders, which gave them the appearance of so many delightful butterflies.

As they approached, I saw that they were all young; not children, but in their early twenties or perhaps a little less, and all were fair skinned and blue eyed as I was. All had curly golden hair; that of the men cut short, while the women wore theirs upswept, with little fringes, and ringlets hanging down at the back. They seemed to be expecting me, and ran and danced around me, their coloured robes forming a kaleidoscope of petals, a delicious human bouquet.

Still laughing and talking, they lifted me and bore me away, back up the steps of the magnificent building from which they had come. I passed beneath the portico and through a gigantic doorway into a huge reception room. It

41

seemed very grand, much grander than any palace on earth. Enormously high white marble columns supported the roof, and at the far end, I caught a glimpse of gold. At first I thought it must be a statue, but as I was borne nearer, I saw that it was a towering golden throne, flanked by great golden statues of goddesses with upswept wings. Set on a high marble dais, it was an incredibly splendid sight.

I was carried up the steps of the dais and seated on the throne, my bare feet dangling. A chaplet of golden leaves was placed upon my curls, and great garlands of flowers, heaps and heaps of them, were brought and set before me. I felt very grand. There I sat in utter splendour, high above the throng, looking down at them. The colours, the spectacle; all was tremendous. How you welcome me. It was the most wondrous sensation, and I sat there feeling almost drunk with it.... The picture faded.

My teachers had made their point. I had questioned them on the sameness of their teachings, and they had given me what I asked to see, a pure confection, something that would not have been out of place on the lips of Scheherezade herself. A tale to amuse and deceive, something with which to fritter away the ticking boredom of time, but with no substance; no fulfilment.

The city was of sugar icing; the clothes and colours were of fondant icing. The people were all young adults; there were no children and no elderly people. It was a city of eternal youth; beautiful, unchanging, and totally false. It contained no nourishment for the spirit; just appeasement of the senses. Quickly my euphoria vanished, leaving me empty and desolate, despondent and out of sorts. Had I been a child, I would have been on the brink of throwing a tremendous temper tantrum.

All my previous pictures had left me with the most wonderful sense of well being, of fulfilment, of rightness. This one did not. I was left chastened and sad, but I learned not to question my teachers.

Months passed and the pictures continued, although they now became far less frequent, leaving me much time to reflect upon their hidden meanings. I was however still puzzled as to what they were, and what was happening to me. I felt that I stood alone; that I must be the only person in the whole world to experience such happenings. My spiritual reassurances continued, but I longed to have some human person, someone at my level, to explain them to me; someone who had trodden the same path before me, to tell me all was well. I needed affirmation and reassurance very badly, and prayed long and hard to my Lord to send someone.

At last my prayers were answered, in a most extraordinary way. I have often noticed that help comes from the direction I least expect. And so it proved.

On a sleepy Sunday evening in the autumn of 1986, I just happened to be watching a TV programme. Filmed at St Beuno's in North Wales, it was about retreats. At the word "retreat," I pricked up my ears. I had always longed to make a retreat, and perhaps find teachers able to help me. The presenter was a Jesuit priest, Father Gerard Hughes. As I listened, I immediately felt a kinship with him and his helpers, and wanted to go there to meet them. But more was to come. He was talking about the Spiritual Exercises of St Ignatius, when suddenly he said the words that I had been waiting for, as though he was talking to me personally;

directing them straight at me!

"Step into the picture!" he.said. "In your meditative state, build a picture and step into it. Become at one with the picture. Take part in it."

*This was exactly what I had been doing all these months.* In the programme, others were being shown how to do this, learning, working at it, while I had been given this gift without asking.

It was as though a thousand candles had been lit in my room; the light and radiance from them filled it, and filled me too. I listened with every atom of my being; every part of me came alive as I drank in every word. Here was a man that I must talk to; I must. As the programme ended, I became on fire with St Ignatius and his teachings.

I spent that night in a fever of anticipation, barely able to wait for morning. As early as I reasonably could, I reached for the telephone, and with hasty fingers, dialled directory enquiries. A new quest had begun. Soon I was speaking to Sister Kathleen at St Beuno's. I told her about the pictures that I had been receiving, and the immensity of Our Lord in my life, and how I was coping with my incapacity and the long days of suffering. Sister Kathleen was so kind and understanding. She spoke to me as though she knew me personally.

"It's all right now, Dorothy," she said. "We've found you, and you have found us. It's all right now. Don't look any further. You have us. You are safe. We've got you now."

She then gave me a telephone number for Father Hughes. Overcome with emotion, I wept; tears of sheer relief.

As luck would have it, Father Hughes himself answered

the phone. This, I was later to learn, was a rare occurrence, as he was very elusive, often out, and very busy when he was in. I started by telling him how much I had enjoyed the programme, then told him all about myself and my experiences. He questioned me closely, I think to ascertain whether or not I was a victim of self-delusion, but I think what really convinced him was how I felt when I came out of the picture. I told him of my feelings of wonderment, of pleasure and joy, and that they left me warm and fulfilled, and stayed with me long afterwards.

Gerry, as I later came to know him, soon confirmed that I was on the right track, much to my delight. He told me that I had unknowingly entered on the Ignatian Spiritual Exercises, and that where others had to work at them, I had been given them quite naturally. My feeling of wellbeing on leaving the picture was just as it should be, according to St Ignatius. This was the start of an excellent friendship.

Contact with Gerry gave me the human affirmation that I had so long sought, and opened a multitude of doors. At last I belonged somewhere. He was unable to come and see me himself, but arranged for others to do so. The first was Sister Pia, of the Institute of the Blessed Virgin Mary, and shortly after, an Anglican vicar who was also a mystic and who ran retreats. Knowing where I belonged and what I was doing enabled me to branch out on my own. I felt like a lotus that had climbed up through the murky water into the sunshine and spread its petals.

I confided in my devout Christian friend, who was very interested, and it was she who told me of a convent only a few miles away, called The Hermitage. This was a very small house with only three or four Sisters, of the Society of the Precious Blood, an Anglican community with its mother house at Burnham Abbey. As soon as she had left, I reached for the telephone. A firm friendly voice answered; that of Sister Jean Mary.

She was marvellous. She heard me out with such love and understanding as I poured out my overwhelmed heart to her. As I finished, she said:

"Well, we are here for you now too, and if you would like to send us some of your tapes, we would be so pleased to listen to them."

Hastily I made copies of a few and bundled them up for Mark to deliver. On his return, I bombarded him with questions. Who had he seen; what did they look like; what was The Hermitage like? Typical man, full of his own preoccupations, he noticed little on that first visit!

The first response to my tapes came by letter from The Hermitage. They had been greatly enjoyed, and this started me on a new course. I had had a message from God, and I wanted to share it with simply everybody. I contacted convent after convent, making many dear friends in the process, and out flew my prayer picture tapes in all directions. Among many others they went to Fr William Hewitt SJ in London; while Minster Abbey had a library of prayer tapes, and received mine gladly. Over the next year they went simply everywhere; even to America, taken by a visiting Sister. Some too went into ordinary homes, to anyone and everyone who wished to hear them, to the poorly and the sick, who said that they were helped by them. Finally some even went to Rome itself, to the Vatican, and among my most treasured possessions are letters from Pope John Paul, and Fr Peter-Hans Kolvenbach, the Superior General of the Society of Jesus. This response was a great joy to me; it was a miracle in my life. Thus God, in His supreme love, answered me.

It is hard to find words to describe what all this meant to me. I felt a supreme exaltation that at last I had work to do. No longer were my talents hidden away; they were being used, as the parable told us they must be. Trusting my Lord utterly, I let everything He wished to give tumble into me, and then back out on to tape. Sometimes I asked, "Have I got that right?", only to be told "Let be; let be." With this I immediately felt at peace.

Meanwhile I stayed in touch with my dear Sister Jean Mary, and we became the closest of friends, although as the order is an enclosed one, we have rarely been able to meet. When she was not able to come to the telephone, I talked to the other sisters, Mary Lawrence, Mary John and Mary Peter, and from time to time, others from the mother house, each of gave to me in her own special way. Precious Blood is a contemplative order, and in many ways I felt a part of it. By now I felt that I truly belonged to so many places that it was hard to remember that only a short time before I had felt that I belonged nowhere.

A friend who had heard some of my tapes told me of a nun who was giving Lenten lectures on stepping into the picture at Westminster Abbey. Hastily I telephoned the Abbey and spoke to a priest, who gave me a telephone number for her. In no time at all I was speaking to her about the lectures, and all that was implied. She was Sister Teresa Margaret of the Convent of the Holy Name; a teaching order. T-M, as she was popularly known, showed the utmost interest, and asked to hear some of my tapes.

She also became a very dear friend. My Lord was sending all these special people into my life to give me their affirmation and their blessings. I shall never cease to thank Him.

By now the prayer pictures were coming many weeks apart. My deep contemplative prayer continued each morning, and this was illuminated for me by the radiance of God and of Christ. I saw many wonderful and mystical things at these times, the Holy Trinity, and the Holy Mother too, of which my soul will speak when the time comes.

I did however receive one series of prayer pictures; this was unique, as normally each was individual and complete. One morning as I entered the picture, I found myself in a large sort of aisle. It had a marble floor stretching away into the distance like a wondrous road bridging infinity, and was flanked by very tall marble columns on either side. Outside all was just space, just light, a very even light, coming from anywhere and everywhere, and from no particular place.

As I wondered what would happen next, a royal blue carpet edged with gold appeared from nowhere at my feet. It unrolled, slowly at first, then faster and faster until it too stretched away into the distance. I stepped forward on to it and looked at it. As I did so, I seemed to look down upon myself. I was wearing a bridal gown. The material was like nothing that I have ever seen on this earth. Of some strange spun stuff, it drifted around me as I walked, rather than actually being worn as a garment. On my head was a wreath of flowers. I felt that I was a bride, but to whom? I knew not. Alone, I walked graciously down this

48

magnificent aisle for a long, long way. The picture faded....

The very next morning, I again found myself walking along the never-ending royal blue carpet, through the aisle of marble columns. Again I walked and walked. Still I was alone. Still there was no sign of what was to come.

The third morning found me still walking, straight down the centre of the endless blue carpet, passing column after column to left and right. Suddenly I felt impelled to move over to my left, and I knew then that another was coming; I was to be joined on my journey. At my side appeared a horse and rider. The horse was the most beautiful rich chestnut colour, while the rider was a knight in full armour. I could not see his face, for his visor was down, but two great plumes waved above his helmet; one deep yellow, the other a dark orangey red. The saddle cloth of the horse was divided; half was deep blue with silver fleur-de-lys, the other the same orangey red of the plume, with golden acorns.

"Who are you?" I asked. There was no answer. Just "Walk," the silence broken only by the hooves of the horse, muffled by the thick blue carpet.

"Who are you?" A companion, I felt. A companion to take me to my own spiritual wedding. Somewhere a feast awaited. I must just keep walking ahead. Keeping perfect step, on we walked, on and on for what seemed like days, feeling neither tired nor cold nor hungry. I felt completely at peace, and certain that this was the right way to do the things that would be asked of me.

On the fourth day, my silent companion and I were still walking along the blue-carpeted aisle, which yet stretched limitlessly ahead. With a smile in my voice, I asked again of the mysterious stranger: "Who are you?"

At last he turned his head and lifted his visor. I found myself looking into the laughing face of a most handsome young man. He had a moustache, and a small pointed beard, and the brownest, merriest laughing eyes that I had ever seen. He spoke.

"I have come to take you to the Master," were his words.

"Oh," I said, with the laughter in my voice implying that this was some wondrous fairy tale. "Do I ride upon your horse?" He laughed down at me, and did not answer in words, but I felt a gentle urging, "Walk on, walk on."

The picture finally faded. For four consecutive mornings I had walked down that endless aisle, on the rich blue and gold carpet, at first alone, and then with a companion who had been sent to escort me, and who I felt I knew. Later, in prayer, I asked who he was. I was told that he was St Ignatius of Loyola.

# CHAPTER 3

# Prayer pictures

For want of a better name, I called my early experiences prayer pictures, partly because I invariably received them while in a state of deep contemplative prayer, and partly because I was, as Gerry Hughes had confirmed, stepping into the picture. In all I received nearly fifty of them in just over eighteen months. The content of many was obscure, with no evident religious theme.

Over and over I was told to look for the word in the picture, and this I did. Often it was difficult to find, but it was always there if I searched long enough and hard enough. Not that they were in any way intellectual puzzles; it was more a matter of waiting for light to dawn rather than unravelling clues. For this reason I have not always commented on the examples given. To me, the biggest mystery was why I felt impelled to record them, but when I started to send out copies, and received people's reactions, I at last understood.

Sometimes the things I was shown prompted my curiosity, and I wanted to know more. Where relevant, I started to ring up people who might know the answers. To give but one example, in The Mechanical Butterfly, I saw gold of a greenish hue. The British Museum confirmed that in ancient times there was such a thing, and that it was highly prized.

There follows a selection of transcripts from the prayer picture tapes. The choice was difficult, but generally these seem to me to be the most important, for a variety of reasons. Not knowing how long they would continue, I did not think to record the dates on which they were received until much later, by which time they had become infrequent. The examples in this section are therefore not necessarily in the order in which they were received, although dates are given where known.

## *MY LADY*

After prayer this morning, I asked my Lord, "Did I truly see Absolom and Ayesha, or were they figments of my imagination?" I was told yes, I indeed do see them. I was told to believe; to believe in myself. After this confirmation, my eyes still closed, I was urged forward into blank space. I drifted, and a picture began to form around me.

On my right was a great clump of palm trees, with green vegetation at its foot, and in front of me was water; an oasis. But it was not ordinary water; it was crystal clear, of the most beautiful aquamarine colour. The urge to touch it, to ruffle its surface, was irresistible. I knelt, and cupping my right hand, dipped it into the lovely aquamarine water. It felt wondrously cool, lighter and clearer than any water on earth. I lifted my hand, expecting it to contain water the same colour as that in the pool. It did not. The water was

52

diamond bright. Liquid diamonds dripped from my fingers. I was urged to lift it to my lips and drink.

Before I could do so, a great light shone, as though the sun had come out in my room. My eyelids were closed, yet still I could see it. The diamond-bright liquid trickled through the fingers of my cupped hand, and I realized that it was growing hot. My palm was hot; the water itself was hot. The heat grew scalding; almost painful, and as I watched, vapour appeared, pluming upwards from the brilliant diamonds in my hand.

Slowly the vapour plume grew and grew, until it was far taller than I, and from within the vapour came a flower. A lily, white and waxen. It was not an Arum lily, but another, whose name I cannot recall; beautiful, pure white with a long green stalk, growing upwards from the palm of my hand. I stood there in awe of it; in wonder at it, and rather frightened by it. Then as I watched, it changed.

It now became a woman in white robes trimmed with gold. I knew immediately who She was. She was divine; She was our Holy Mother. I knelt and grovelled, pressing my forehead against the earth, fearful and trembling, yet full of love; unbelievable love and wonder and amazement. I dared not think of it; it was inconceivable, and still is, long afterwards, that She should appear; first guised as a lily, then as a woman in white robes trimmed with gold, and golden sandals on slim bare feet. She was beautiful, with a smooth alabaster complexion, eyes the deepest sapphire blue, and dark honey coloured hair under a pure white headcloth trimmed with brilliant gold.

She smiled down at me; a sweetly curving smile full of gentleness and loving tenderness. There was strength in

53

her smile too, and courage. The diamond brilliance surrounded us, and I was part of the brilliance. She came from the centre of my palm, which seemed to have grown to giant size. How strange, that She and I were one; of the same body, for She grew from me and I grew from Her. I spoke to Her in a trembling voice.

"O Lady, Lady of all the Heavens, I have spoken to You so often. I'm a trembling child, fearful yet loving, loving beyond the confines of this earth. I love Thee; Thou art here. Thou tellest me that this oasis is a place of rest and rejuvenation. I have many things to do on this earth; many things to do with this frail and feeble body. I am to be made strong to do the work of our Holy Lord. In wonder I listen; trembling I hear O Lady. Thou touchest me, and in Thy touch I am renewed and I tremble in the rebirth. Trembling, consumed with love, light and brilliance, I love Thee."

. * * * * *

Long after I recorded this tape I am still trembling. I find it inconceivable that this actually happened to me. But of course it did. Even though I have returned to the world, and am sitting up drinking tea, the oasis is still around me. I still feel the wetness of the water, and She is still here with me. I am in two worlds; the material world, and yet very much of the spiritual world at the same time. I asked:

"What is this all about? What will become of me? What am I to do with all this? Is it for me alone, or am I to tell others?"

I am told to go forward now, and all things will come to me. All things, miraculous, mystical, enchanting, wonderful

54

things shall be shown me. When the time comes, I shall know what to say, and how to write, of these wonders.

## THE MECHANICAL BUTTERFLY

Prayer was difficult this morning. The old familiar feeling of longing to get out and about swept over me, making me restless and fretful. My mind kept wandering. Then the picture formed.

It started with a box-shaped parcel, wrapped in the old-fashioned way with brown paper, tied with a pink silk ribbon with a large bow on the top. Parcels have always intrigued me, and I longed to see inside.

At a silent command, the ribbon slid prettily undone, and curled against the base of the parcel. Then the brown paper started to unwrap itself, revealing a large cardboard box with a close-fitting lid, the type of box common fifty years ago, but now rarely seen. Slowly the lid rose, then it slipped to one side. I could feel my excitement mounting as I peered in.

At first, all I could see was tissue paper. Then it rustled, and slowly parted. I wondered what on earth was going to appear. And what did appear greatly surprised me. A large butterfly emerged from the tissue. It rose clumsily from the box and then, with strange, jerky wing movements, flew around the room. I realised that it was a mechanical butterfly, a clockwork butterfly.

It was a beautiful thing. Its body was made of a rare greeny gold, finely detailed. The wings were peacock blue with small irridescent green patterns, edged with the same greeny gold as the body. It flew so stiffly and strangely, yet looked so lovely, like an exquisite toy; a Fabergé plaything. Astounded, I asked: "Why a mechanical butterfly?"

I was told that the butterfly had been imprisoned in the box for a very long time, and that to preserve itself, it had had to change its substance. A fragile living creature would soon have died and crumbled into dust, but by changing itself into metal of the most precious kind, it continued to exist, and retained its perfection for many long years.

This made tremendous sense to me. But the precious butterfly that I now saw belonged in a glass cabinet. It was not free to live among the flowers of earth. Must it stay in its box? I asked if it would change again.

I was told that now the lid had come off and it was free, it would change again, and adapt to a new environment where it could once more live and breath. At last it could slough off its metal exterior, and become fragile and soft-winged again; part of the living world, among the flowers, sipping their nectar. This beautiful thing, which had been released before my eyes, would change into a lovely living butterfly, after all those years shut away unseen.

In this I saw that my psyche, dormant during years of being trapped in my ailing body, hemmed in by frustrations, had changed its nature in order to survive, but now having been released, could now fly free again. Similarly I saw that the church, in times of adversity, survived by surrounding itself with bright and shining pomp and ritual, ready to emerge and live again when the right time came.

56

## ON THE HILL (April 1986)

My Lord wore heavy robes today, of a thick, off-white material, wrapped around His head and shoulders. I wondered why. I stood holding His left hand, as we looked out over the uneven, rocky ground. Shimmering in the distance, a city appeared, a city built of white stone and guarded by a strong white stone wall. The hill we stood upon was quite high, and from it I could see down into the city. In the centre was a holy place, surmounted by a huge golden dome, which shone brightly in the sunlight. For a moment I saw a cross upon it, but even as I looked, it vanished, leaving the dome smooth.

I turned to my Lord to ask about this shimmering white city, and realized that I was looking up at Him. Up and up. This was a strange feeling, for I am very tall, and more used to looking down at people. I realized that I had become a child again.

I saw myself as a child. I was no more than four years old, with brown curls tumbling loosely across my forehead, wearing a short tunic down to my knees, revealing sturdy young legs, tanned and brown from playing for long hours in the sun, and scratched here and there as if by thorns. My calves had almost baby curves, and on my feet were sandals. I knew instantly that I was a boy. I was the same gender as this man at my side, whom I called Lord.

I felt a fierce love for Him; He was all things to me: father, brother, much-loved family friend, all rolled into one. I felt safe and loving and loved in His presence, and enjoyed His company so much.

Looking towards the city again, I saw huge grey storm clouds gathering. They hung over it, darkening still more, obliterating the sun, casting it into heavy shadow. It grew colder. I sensed that the most awful storm was coming, and that there was going to be torrential rain. Now I knew why my Lord was so warmly dressed.

In the city wall was a great archway, deep in shadow. I could not see the gate, but somehow knew that it was open. As I watched, a pathway started to form, leading from the archway to where we stood. Of the same white stone as the city wall, it was just wide enough for the two of us. We set out, with me holding tightly to my Lord's hand as I skipped happily alongside Him.

The skies grew ever darker and heavy laden as we approached the wall, although we could still see quite easily. We reached the archway. No-one was there to greet us or to join our company, and we entered the city alone. As I passed the gate, I grew from being a boy, into a young woman, about sixteen or seventeen years old. My boy's tunic became a pretty gown, at first white, then flushed with pink. The colour was that of a rose in a previous prayer picture, and I knew by this that I was dressed in Peace.

With this transformation, my hand parted from that of my Lord. I did not feel afraid at this; it just seemed right at the time. Nor did I feel alarmed when I noticed that my Lord was now nowhere to be seen, although I had not noticed His going.

I was very excited at being in the city. I had expected to see people, but the streets were deserted and it was all terribly quiet. Now that I was within the city instead of looking down on it, I saw that it was a jumble of streets and alleyways and turnings. I was about to say "Oh, this is a maze," but I was told "No, a labyrinth."

The sky began to clear, and soon the sun shone brightly, reflecting back the white brilliance that I had seen shimmering in the distance. The high walls around me prevented me from seeing the great golden dome of the holy place, but I knew that I had to find my way to it. I felt the desire to run, and sped down the byways and alleys, through streets and giant squares, seeking, always seeking, the centre of the labyrinth.

Suddenly I felt an air of expectancy and anticipation, from a crowd that I could not see. There were still lots of streets and alleys that I had to travel along to reach the holy place, and I could feel a great hubbub of noise, of excitement rising: "Someone's coming, someone's coming!" On I sped, my feet light as a whisper, beautifully dressed, as though for a party; very happy and light as any young maid would feel going to such an exciting place at such an exciting time. Who was to come? Who was to come?

The picture dimmed and disappeared, leaving me still full of expectancy and anticipation, wanting so much to become part of the throng; to receive whoever was going to appear. Perhaps one day I shall return.

## THE CUSTODIAN OF THE KEEP

The darkness was almost inky black, with just a faint blue light by which I saw a shape begin to form. I saw wings first, in the centre of the picture, just dark wings.

"Is it a butterfly?" I asked, "Or a bird?"

But even as I spoke, I saw that the wings were not butterfly-shaped. Nor were they moving. In the inky blackness, the faint blue luminosity, reminding me of a fitful moon peering through cloudy skies, spread across the wings, allowing me to see them a little more clearly. The dark shape came closer, and I saw that it was a strange bird, the like of which I had never seen before. As it loomed before me, I thought, "It's an eagle. It's an eagle!" But it was not an eagle. It was immense; colossal. I could not believe my eyes. It was beyond all that I had ever seen, even in a story book, a mythical bird. I had never seen a bird of such size.

"You are not an eagle," I said. "You are a Phoenix."

I do not know what made me say this; it was the last thing I would have thought of, for an eagle is the most majestic bird that I am familiar with.

This great mythical bird hung low in the darkness, showing me, with his magnificent wingspan, that he was so large that he could span whole continents. I saw whole continents, the lands of the earth, pass under his mightily beating wings as he flew low over them, travelling slowly, as though he was protecting all upon earth. This magnificent bird would fly to a clarion call of need, he would come as though to a battle trumpet.

I knew nothing of his ways, and yet I knew deep in my heart what he was and what he stood for. For the first time I knew him. He has been upon this earth, and been of service to man, since long before recorded history. He is associated with ancient Greece, but he appeared on earth long before those times.

Phoenix is the foe of adversity. He will take the sword of adversity from it and smite it down with its own weapon, to regain those lands of which he is the keeper. He is a custodian of the keep. I do not understand these words. The custodian of the keep. Phoenix, I see you, you show me your power. You were made for earth, and you come to us all in adversity, great adversity. When you hear our call you come. When we are struck down and crushed by the mighty blows of an enemy, you will come and smite him, and restore order and rebirth and renewal. You will come in time of great famine, plague; whatever great misfortune hits this earth you will come. And you have come to show me yourself. I am honoured and privileged to see you.

I try to gauge your height, how strange we humans are. We have to try to bring everything into proportion, for us to understand. You stand before me, far bigger than a pyramid. Why a pyramid, why not a mountain? I am smaller than the smallest of your great talons. I look up to your head. It is eagle-like, yet not, with a great hooked beak. Your enormous topaz yellow eye, burning and all-seeing, blinks slowly at me. The pupil is blacker than night, blacker than the deepest space in the heavens. It is as timeless as the universe, and I am in awe of you. While I know that you are a friend, your magnificence brings fear to me.

Your feathers are strange. As I look at them, they are not soft feathers. They are hard, and they lay against your neck in a perfect symmetry of pattern. I realize that no wind could ruffle those feathers, for they are of bronze. You have turned yourself into bronze. This is tremendously difficult to understand.

Why bronze? You have turned yourself into a god. People have worshipped you as a god, and they fashioned

61

you in bronze, a symbol carried upon the shields or breastplates of warriors. You have been cast in many guises; to lead an army, to be worshipped. Phoenix, you show yourself in bronze to me, as a shield, a pennon, a symbol. You are mysterious. I do not fully understand what I have seen. And yet I am filled with your mighty strength. Phoenix, I want to know all there is about you. You have much to teach me. I shall seek to know you.

## THE SUMMER RESIDENCE (June 1986)

The sun was hot, yet not uncomfortably so. All around were olive trees, their branches and trunks so gnarled and twisted, in contrast to the rather pretty silvery green leaves, and its abundant fruit. The olive tree has always seemed to symbolize so much of myself. My face is pleasing like the leaves, while the abundant fruit is the abundance of love I have, while my leg is ugly, like an olive bough.

I was wearing a kimono-style dress with wide sleeves, of a blush pink colour. It was of a light, soft fabric which shone like satin, and was beautifully cool. My hair was pulled high upon my head in a kind of bun, and I could feel a delicious cool breeze around the nape of my neck. In bed, my neck is always trapped against my pillow, and my hair sticks to it with perspiration. It has been so long since I felt a cool breeze on the back of my neck.

My hands were outstretched, and a heavy weight was placed in them. This morning, before prayer, I had wished to bring a gift for my Lord. This was it, but I had no idea what it could be. I looked. It was a large and beautifully carved dish of dark wood, smooth but not highly polished, piled high with gloriously coloured fruit. Dark purple plums; ripe peaches warm in their own sweetness; apples, oranges, all clustered round a centrepiece of pineapples. Juicy green and black grapes lined the rim, and dripped over in places.

My Lord was standing nearby, wearing a cream linen robe, and a headcloth, which he does not always wear. He was young; in His early thirties, His lean face deeply tanned from outdoor living, and shining dark brown hair, worn long and slightly curly, as was His beard. He was surrounded by His followers, all in robes of different hues. Carrying my enormous dish of fruit, I walked towards Him, feeling the beaten earth warm under my bare feet. I was full of pleasure at what I was about to give Him.

He gave me a discerning look. His eyes were clear and very blue as they gazed directly into mine. Such a penetrating gaze I had never before known. I knew that although He was looking at the exterior face that I show the world, they pierced the mask to see the innermost me; the hidden me, the very core of my being. I felt rather uncomfortable at this; almost an intruder, but stared back at Him, eager to please Him, my love for Him shining from me. In His eyes, as well as love I could see a searching. I also knew that they could show anger; He is not all the meek and mild and loving Lord we are so often told about. He has a great sense of justice, and if He was displeased with what we were doing, He would make His displeasure felt in no uncertain manner.

I was not to see that side of Him this morning. Thank heavens! Instead I experienced the calm and giving and peaceful Lord; the loving Lord. I hunched down, bending both knees, and placed the dish of fruit at His feet. Then I won my smile from Him. It filled me with joy, and lifted my heart and spirit more than I can tell in words. In that smile I felt new-born and alive as though for the first time. Always I get this sense of renewal from my Lord.

Turning, He gestured to His followers. A young boy came forward and picked up my dish, carrying it proudly. My Lord turned and walked off through the olive grove. We all followed.

And so I followed Him, walking on two perfect legs, with such joyous freedom, freedom from pain. We walked on, through the green surrounding countryside in the bright sunshine of early morning, until at last we came upon a dwelling, modest in size. The front of it was arched in the Moorish style, and looking closely as we entered, I saw it was made of white marble. The words came to me as we entered its shady interior, this is a summer residence.

As I crossed the threshold, I saw that the inside was quite huge, far bigger than the modest exterior had suggested. The marble floor was deliciously smooth and cool to my bare feet. There were no rugs; just low wooden benches, ornately carved by clever hands, and spilling over them were large silken cushions, of a blush pink colour like my dress. Corded around the edges with thick gold braid, and with gold tassels at their corners, they were exquisite.

Looking around, I noticed for the first time that although the floor and ceiling were of plain white marble, the walls were not plain. One long continuous frieze was painted all the way around them, with life sized figures of what I can only call angels, with wings and fair flowing hair, set against a wonderful celestial blue background. They wore floaty gowns of unbelievable colours, and as I gazed at them, I realized that I was surrounded by the colours of the fruits that I had brought my Lord; dark purples, peaches, yellows, oranges, reds of every description, greens of the palest hues; all were there. The angels were clothed in them.

They all carried musical instruments. Some had harps, and other things that I could not put a name to, while others were blowing conch-shell trumpets. I could actually hear the sounds that they were making. They were truly vibrating the music out of the frieze as I watched. It was very strange, and even harder to describe. I felt that at any moment these angel figures would start marching around the walls, so lifelike were they. A blink of an eye and it could happen. The colours breathed life into them, making them appear to quiver, even as the glowing fruits lived within their dish.

My Lord had accompanied me in, and was standing by my side, although his followers had remained outside. It was so absolutely wonderful to be there with Him. My companion, dearest to me in all the world. All too soon the picture faded.

In receiving my gift, my Lord had given me insight, another great gift, in return. This happens throughout my life; as I give to Him, so I receive. This is the wonder and beauty of it all. You can never give a gift, much as you long to, without receiving a gift back. Someone's immense pleasure at your gift shines from their face, and you receive their delight, their gift back to you. It happens every time, and it doesn't have to be Christmas. It could be the smallest gift; a single flower, perhaps even a word to make them laugh. But always in giving, one receives.

## THE BRINGER OF PEACE

Dawn, the beginning of a new day. The lower half of the houses were in darkness, although I could make out streets and alleyways. The doors were all firmly shut, and the town was deep in sleep. Far in the distance a cock crew, his voice heralding a new day, but all else was quiet. Then the silence was broken by the rumble of wheels, and a cart appeared from a side turning and came towards my Lord and me. It was drawn by a donkey, a small, sturdy donkey with a rough grey woolly coat, lovely chunky face with a white muzzle, and a blaze of white up his nose.

The cart was roughly hewn. No real craftsman had made it, just a man who knew his job, and did it quickly and cheaply. It was a good solid cart. The wheels were solid wooden rounds which bumped slightly over the uneven ground.

The donkey pulled it effortlessly. Everything was calm and full of joy about him. I could make a pet of this little donkey. At first he seemed quite alone, happily trundling through the streets, but then I saw a man at his side. He wore a warm woollen cloak, and I knew than that daybreak must be quite cold. The cloak was dark grey, with other colours woven into it. His robe was white, as was his headcloth, held with two round cords. On his feet were sandals. He and his donkey were good companions

66

together through the darkened streets. Everyone else was fast asleep.

Always curious, I peered into the back of the cart to see what it carried. Some sort of farm produce, vegetables, or fruit, I guessed, for I thought the donkey must be taking his wares to market. In the back of the cart were sacks of rough material, tied at the necks with twine. There must have been four or five in all, filled to the top. I wondered what they contained. Perhaps it was grain, but no, how could it be grain? This was a very large town; there were no fields here. So dismissing the idea of grain, I wondered again what it could be. It really did bother me that I did not know. I turned to my Lord and asked Him: "Do you know what is inside these sacks?"

He did not reply, but the answer came immediately. One sack untied itself, and under my incredulous gaze, a whole flock of doves flew out. Surely this cannot be, I thought; doves coming from a sack! They flew gloriously, free, high into the air, not looking at all crushed or subdued by their time inside the sack, but round and round, white and plump and beautiful, eyes shining, in absolutely peak condition. After a while, they perched on the rooftops. Some sat alone, while others huddled together, and they began their morning cooing, greeting the new day. They looked so lovely, I wanted to reach out and touch them. But doves from a sack—what did this mean? I thought and thought it over, for it did not seem to make sense.

Doves signify peace and hope, and peace and hope come from many strange and unexpected places. The start of every new day is a new beginning in our lives, and new beginnings always bring new hope, even in war-torn cities or in terrible sorrows. Troubled times will pass. No matter how dreadful, and how awful situations are, the doves of peace and hope settle on the roofs of all our houses. Did the man with his donkey and cart travel through the streets and byways of all lands, bringing peace and hope at the break of every new day? For those who seek, peace is there. God bless the Prince of Peace. Reach out your hands and your hearts to Him, and you will find peace. It means seeking hard, and sometimes despairing, as I myself well know, but I have known for a long time that peace does exist within oneself.

This picture would not leave me, and during the day, I found that I was forming new thoughts. The house doors were shut tight, as I thought, in slumber, but in these pictures, often all is not what it seems. Looking deeper, as I have always been told to do, perhaps those doors were closed and bolted from within from fear. Perhaps the town had been under some form of siege, or awful tyranny. That on this morn, the tyranny had left it, and the people would soon feel the unfamiliar quietness and peace for the first time, and would open their doors and see for themselves that the feeling of occupation, of fear, had been removed. Then they could go about their business of living once more.

I thought of the many wars that have been fought, the young lives wasted, the young blood spilt and soaking into the soil. In time, all things pass: war, plague, famine. Returning now to the battlefields of old, we see grasslands or cornfields, skylarks hovering in the air and singing. The memories of war have faded, and peace has returned.

## GREEN GLASS, THE BEGINNING

This morning I stepped into the picture at my Lord's side. We were in a dry and arid landscape, with strange rock formations hidden beneath a thick layer of dust. Not sand, not earth, but a strange clogging dust. The dust of centuries, of millions of centuries, coated the surface. A hot dry wind blew ferociously but silently about us, whipping at our clothes.

I immediately felt curious to know what lay beneath the dust, and bent down to feel the rocks beneath it. As I stretched my fingers towards one of the nearer lumps, the wind blew even harder, an intense jetstream of wind, low past my feet. It started to move the thick dust, which lifted heavily, great plumes of it blowing thick on the wind. As it went, I began to see what lay beneath it.

I bent down to look closely, my hands brushing away the last of the dust. The surface was cool to the touch, and I saw that far from being rock, it was made of dark green glass, gleaming dustily. How extraordinary! It was rather similar to the glass of medicine bottles which I had seen as a child, but darker and denser. Here and there it looked almost black, but from most angles I could see that it was dark green. The entire terrain was of glass, or of a mineral very similar.

Soon all the dust had gone. The wind dropped, leaving us in a strange still landscape. It was not smooth and even; there were lumps and boulders, ravines, and high cliffs of glass. It was like some form of Arctic land, but with dark green glass instead of white ice. I stepped carefully, but it was not sharp to my feet, nor slippery, but strangely ridged to walk upon. What on earth was it, I wondered. I said to my Lord,

"What on earth has happened? Is it the sea, trapped here forever, its motion petrified? Is it some spell or enchantment? Why this?"

My Lord said nothing, but I always get thoughts and feelings from Him. "Wait. Wait, and all will be revealed." And so it was to be. Time seemed to fly by, and I continued on, scrambling up the sides of this cool dark green glass, never slipping or losing my balance, but picking my way carefully.

After what seemed ages, the surface of the glass began to break up. It split asunder with a loud cracking noise. Great fissures opened, and huge shards of glass splintered away from each other like ice, forming great dark floes of green glass. As they floated apart, I could see at last see what lay beneath. It was light. The most brilliant light started to shine through.

Soon the floes melted and were gone. I was alone with the light, for my Lord had also disappeared. There was no sky. There had been no sky at the beginning. There seemed no use for a sky. I felt it hadn't been invented yet.

To my shock, the light became water, still brilliantly luminous. It was quiet and still, and although I could see no shore line, I knew it was a huge lake, and not a sea. Light and water were one, and I was in it, floating and swimming. It was a wonderful feeling, and I was not at all frightened.

This was surprising, for I have never been able to swim, so I ought to have felt fear. Then I dared it to drown me. I had a feeling: go, deep under the water, have courage, go! I dived deep, deep into this brilliant water. Of course it didn't drown me. I found an element that I had never before experienced. I was swimming in water. I swam beautifully, instinctively, round and round, up and down, in complete freedom. I did a perfect underwater ballet, such as I had seen in films, rejoicing and glorying in the delight of movement. It was breathtaking.

I bobbed up to the surface again, and tried to splash the water, but to my surprise it would not splash. I gathered some up in my hands and threw it, expecting to see a cascade of sparkling droplets, but no, it did not happen. My handfuls of water left my palms in huge misshapen balls that fell in on themselves, forming and settling themselves into great globules which hung in midair and floated brightly about me, as water does in space. I pinged them with my finger, and patted them sideways, but they would not break up, but floated gently down, finally plopping into the wholeness from whence they came. I played with them like a child. I did not tire. I felt in my rightful element. I was not lonely, hungry, cold, or frightened.

All at once I had a feeling; hold on, brace yourself, something is about to happen. I stopped playing now, and was quiet and still. My gaze skimmed across the luminous water. Then, in the distance, I saw it. A gigantic blood-red sun started to rise, slowly and majestically, from the water, turning it pink. With the sun came music, magnificent music, welling up from I knew not where. It swelled and swelled about me, singing of the triumph of the new sun[1].

Huge, enormously huge, much larger than our earthly

---

[1] *I learned long afterwards that the music was Ravel's* Daphnis and Chloë Suite 2.

sun, it filled my vision entirely. Its rising, its giant, colossal proportions, the enormity of it, still did not frighten me. Part of me seemed to accompany the sun as it rose; the stirring part of man's soul ascending, the mortal body sending forth the immortal image to the glory of the heavens. I gazed at it, as one might have in olden times, mesmerized at seeing a living god. This was a sun god.

At last the sun cleared the water, and with its rising it brought forth sky, sky that had not existed before. A sky tinged with pinks and mauves, soft yellows and purples. Clouds formed, pink-tinged. Light was coming; soft yellow light. The sun rose high into its own sky, and the clouds were its companions. They hung about it, accompanying it, reflecting its splendour. I had seen the first sunrise, the beginning of light on earth. The wonder of it was indescribable. I was spellbound.

The gigantic luminous lake began to dissolve and sink. Earth was forming now, and the water turned into luminous vapour, like some giant fog, which sank into the new-formed earth, green with new baby shoots, growing and carpeting the land about me.

By now the sun had risen high, and all was as it should be on a new morning. My bare feet stood on new grass, and a mantle of fresh green cloaked the earth. Grasslands and pastures, great trees, forests and jungles. It was the beginning of life. The light shone upon the earth, and the sun warmed it. It was good. I was tired now, and must leave the picture.

Of all my prayer pictures, Green Glass was the most obscure. For years I sought the word in the picture, and only recently have I found it.

Our Lord is mystery, hidden from our mortal eyes and mortal minds. He also exists deep within us, in the divine spark of our souls, but hidden from our normal conscious state. Each of us is at one with the cosmos, and part of it, and so our quest for Him must take us outside ourselves into the cosmos, and deep within ourselves at the same time, for the two are one.

The dust in the picture is cosmic dust, the unknowing and unknowable, the mystery which cloaks all, and conceals the true realities. When we look at the world around us, we see only the dust masking the truth which lies below it. The wind that dispersed the dust was sent by the divine grace of my Lord to clear away the mystery, the layer of unknowing, and help me to see truly.

The green glass is the shell surrounding both us and the world as we see it. It is the shell of the physical world, and of our physical selves, and consists of all the elements that make up the world, the physical laws that govern them, and the beginnings of earthly life. It is also a barrier, separating the world about us from the spiritual world; and our own resistance to our attempts to explore the depths within.

Faith, knowledge, will, and the utter surrender of self, cracked the green glass, allowing me to enter the light within, to penetrate a deeper layer of awareness close to the entrance of the cosmic soul. The water, which was yet brilliant light, was the primordial water of the beginning of time; the water of the womb of the earth, the water from which all things arose, and my swimming in it was the freedom given to the self by union with the soul.

73

The rising of the sun, which is both SUN and SON, is the birth of the world. Both SUN and SON took on a physical presence to make themselves known to mankind. It was also the beginning of mortal time; man-made time, which the immortal soul transcends.

## LAND OF THE BLUEBELLS (Whit Monday 1986)

When I first saw my Lord this morning He was in the distance, striding purposefully ahead. Calling out, and half laughing, I ran after Him, joyous, light of heart and of foot. I ran carefully, wary of stubbing my toes, for I noticed that the ground was very uneven, with pitfalls and quite large rocks. Finally I caught up with Him, and He turned His head a little towards me. In the early pictures I could never see my Lord's face clearly; but I saw His hair; just a bit of it beyond the edge of His headcloth. It was dark brown. Although He remained silent, I was aware he was pleased at my coming, while I was overjoyed to be with Him again.

I had to half trot to keep up with Him. He knew this, but didn't slacken His pace, but still strode on ahead. He was dressed in the familiar cream robe and headcloth, and carried a stout staff in His left hand, which as He walked, He planted down firmly on the rocky surface of the way ahead.

We journeyed on together. He strode with great purpose and determination. He knew where He was going. I did not, but just walked alongside Him, happy to be in His company. Looking around, I saw the terrain. It was rocky,

very rocky, and everything looked dusty, dry and sandy-
coloured. It was very hard to walk on. Only dusty grass
grew, in crevices between the rocks. I don't know how it
grew, for there seemed to be no moisture at all. Little
clumps of dusty grass, looking as thirsty as I was. The sky
was heavy, and sandy coloured too, with not a break in the
thick clouds. Far above them was the sun. I could not see
it, but could feel its heat. The light beneath the clouds
reflected the stony earth over which we walked. It was a
strange light, a barren, arid, sandy, stone-coloured light.
Far, far in the distance, lay hills. They were mauvey
coloured, and a faint light hung above them, edging their
outlines.

Still half-walking, half-trotting, I ran at His side as He
purposefully picked His way between the boulders and
over the smaller rocks, He seemed to have no trouble with
this, although I found it difficult. Soon I began to get tired.
I was stumbling a little, and aware that I was growing very
thirsty. There was no water, no pouch or skin; no flask, and
so the parchedness grew. My lips became dry, mouth dry,
skin dry, and I felt completely dry and uncomfortable.
Dust settled all over me. Dust was on my face, stiffening
it a little. Although growing ever wearier, I was still quite
happy and content to keep up with Him.

It grew more arduous; more difficult to continue. He
seemed to know this; I did not need to call out to tell Him.
He switched His staff to His right hand, and took my hand
in His left. It helped me greatly. My steps became lighter,
and this endless barren land seemed less forbidding. My
hand clasped in His, I walked strongly on, more strongly
than before. On and on we went, seemingly endlessly. I

was growing footsore and weary again, even though I was clasping my Lord's hand. Its slimness and strength, comfort and sureness, was with me. Without it I could not have kept going. What seemed an eternity passed. My eyes were dry now, and burning with dust. The heat was growing uncomfortable. And we all seemed to be quite coated; robes, me, landscape, coated in this parching dust.

As we neared the purple hills, a fierce wind blew, hot and dry, tugging at our robes and pushing us backwards, as though to keep us from our destination. It seemed to want us to stay forever in this region of arid dryness, and perhaps die in it, become a part of it, and turn to dust and stone. By now I was feeling quite at the end of my tether, and wondered, although I dismissed the idea, if my Lord would have to carry me the last few miles. But no, we journeyed on. As I clung to my Lord's hand, He took me there, and no rough terrain, nor wind, nor hot parched dryness and choking dust, could hold us back.

We arrived at our destination at last, and I stumbled into it. It was a completely different world. It was pure lush green, heavy and wet from some recent torrential rainfall, which left the air moist, with that delicious smell of newly washed grass and soil. And to my delight, the purple came to life. Spread before me and beyond me, as far as my eyes could see, was a haze of bluebells. A whole landscape of them, rising over hill and dale. All was wet; the bluebells were wet; the grass that they grew in was wet. Pleasant rivers, heavy and newly swollen with rain flowed, abundant with water. The skies above us were English skies, full of rainclouds, grey and heavy. They had fulfilled their promise of rain. The bluebells were covered with tiny dancing droplets. Everything was crystal bright, all newly washed. The smell of bluebells, of bluebell woods that I knew as a child, rose above me and about me. The delicious fragrance of bluebells. It was all so marvellous. This world, this wonderful world, had somehow survived the arid wasteland around it, and conquered it.

Both of my hands were now clasping my Lord's left hand. I was oh, so glad to be there. I too was quite damp from the atmosphere. Blessed moisture now coated my parched face. My eyes were shining and soothed, as the burning passed away. I was refreshed and invigorated. How precious again the sense of wonder is. Grass, moisture, fragrance; blessed clouds, grey and heavy, a journey from thirst of spirit as well as body, to a land of moisture and beauty. And so I rose above the picture, and saw my Lord and myself standing in this misty, bluey, purpley haze of bluebells, and lush green grass, and looked down upon us both. I leave it now, but the heavy smell of bluebells and rain and grass is still around me as the picture fades.

Back in my bed, I am still surrounded by the delicious smell of bluebells. I feel invigorated, and renewed by this picture. And so I start my day now, of routine. But I am still lost in this bluebell land. It will be with me, all day and forever.

## THE TREASURE HOUSE (1988)

It has been such a long time since I last received a picture; since January in fact. I rather thought that I had lost the art of receiving my Lord's pictures; perhaps I was not pleasing Him in some way. I began to question myself. But then I

77

realized that I had been busy with other things, learning the Jesuit beliefs, which have stood me in such marvellous stead. I have grown a lot since these pictures first started. Then, this afternoon, I was lying quietly on the couch in my living room, when another picture appeared.

I was in a hot, barren and dusty country. Before me lay a cliff face, with a great boulder against it. It reminded me of the boulders used to seal tombs in our Lord's day, but I knew that it did not conceal a tomb, but something else, something hidden from me. Around the boulder clustered a group of men, pulling and tugging at it with all their might. They had fierce, darkly tanned faces and beards, with turbans on their heads, robes, and baggy trousers tucked into their boots. They looked rather like modern Afghan tribesmen. Under their eager hands, the boulder slowly rolled away and crashed on to its side, showing me what lay behind it.

It was the entrance to a passage, high but narrow. I would have expected it to be dark, but no, it was brilliantly lit for me, and I could see it stretching for a great distance. The sides, the ceiling, and the floor were of smooth hard rock. I entered, and the brilliant light travelled with me. I had no other companion. As I moved, the brilliant light moved, and the darkness fled before me.

I did not feel at all frightened, but more interested in my adventure. We walked on, my light and I. After travelling some considerable distance, we came to a great cavern, with a vaulted roof as high as a cathedral. Before me lay smooth water, an underground lake. The water was clear, and faintly luminous, while the cavern itself was lit with a faint bluish light. At the near shore lay a boat, a rather narrow, shallow, but graceful skiff. It had no oars, and no boatman, but I clambered gingerly aboard and sat down. There was no need for such care, as the boat remained solid and secure.

"How will I travel?" I asked myself.

But even as I spoke, the boat edged itself away from the shore and set out across the lake. It travelled in a mysterious fashion. I glanced over the side, and saw little ripples and fingers of water, little frills of water, propelling it.

Gently we nudged against the rocky far shore, and with great dexterity I jumped out. I stood and looked around me. Then I saw a stairway carved in the rock, a stairway with a wooden handrail. At the top was a square door, of plain wooden boards. As I mounted the stairs, it slowly opened for me. I entered.

Inside I was met by a priest, robed in purple and black. His face was oriental. He told me that I could choose any of the treasures within, adding that some of them were worth a king's ransom. Turning, he led the way into a large cave, brightly lit by hundreds, or even thousands, of candles, each burning brighter than our earthly ones.

I gaped. Even Aladdin's cave was never like this. Treasures were everywhere, spilling over tables, piled high on the floor. Gold, diamonds, emeralds, great ropes of pearls; great ewers and figurines made of precious metals and encrusted with gems, giving back the light from the candles in a scintillating display. There were great rolls of wonderful silks and fabrics, and the walls were lined with great paintings; magnificent works of art. Was I really to choose something from all this?

I walked around, lost in wonderment and admiration. I

lingered for a moment before a great golden crucifix, studded with huge rubies, but passed on. But the magnificence was too much for me, and I quickly became sated with it. Just when I was about to give up, I saw in one corner a small wooden table, with barley sugar legs. On it was a plain white porcelain dish, filled with living water. Upon the water floated a perfumed, golden-coloured waterlily. In all that fantastic display, it was the only living thing. I knew instantly that I would choose it. I turned to the old priest. He smiled, and I knew that I had made the right choice. The picture faded. It was the final one.

As time passed, I reflected much upon this picture, for it was mysterious and enchanting. The wait for the hidden entrance to be revealed. The long dark tunnel, narrow and straight, of my quest, with only my interior light to show me the way. Crossing the underground lake; leaving one shore of self to journey to another, more spiritual shore. Entering the treasure house, in which all the immense wealth of earthly kingdoms was laid out for me to choose from. And at last beholding the golden waterlily; the flower hidden in the very core of the soul. The golden flower that men have sought for thousands of years, often in vain; the perfumed flower of the soul of all knowledge, the true treasure amidst the transient magnificence of earth. The most prized holy blossom given to me by my Lord, humbling me, but filling me with exaltation. I thank the Lord Jesus for this greatest of all blessings.

# CHAPTER 4

# The harvest

When the prayer pictures ceased, I entered a time of learning. Certain books were recommended by my Jesuit friends, and during the next few months I read much and learned much. Already I knew that the third eye had opened, and that I was indeed a mystic. I had always expected this to be, but it was lovely to have it confirmed. Constantly I sought affirmation, my greatest need at this time, and I received it in abundance. I read many works by mystical authors, and it was wonderful to meet myself sitting between the pages of a book. At last I had found myself, and I can't tell you how much it meant to me.

I don't really know where the prayer pictures ended and mysticism began, because one is of the other. Part, the most important part, finally becomes the mystical infusion of divine grace; pure spiritual mysticism, given directly in communion with our Lord. In mysticism, this is what happens. You do not go in search of it; it must come to you. It happened to me with the prayer pictures. It was quite sudden. I did not search for them: how could I, as I had no inkling of their existence? They were just given to me. My life became a pursuit of the Living God. It came to me so naturally, although it is very difficult to explain. Everything hinges on "getting to know you," knowledge of our Holy Father.

Although the prayer pictures had ceased, I continued each morning to enter my Lord's grace in prayer, which I now knew to be a joining of souls; a kinship with the Most Holy. At the very beginning, I heard myself say:

"Lord, I will pursue You beyond the reaches of time; further than the most distant star; I will seek You. Hide where You will, I shall find You. For You are mine by right, my Lord God. Your Son the Christ told us this. And now I claim You as my own, and I will chase You through the very heavens themselves and capture You."

At the time of this impassioned plea I did not know that I really would find Him; that in fact He was leading me on; leading me into the dance of the universe. He made me want Him with every fibre of my being; made me desire Him more than anything on earth or in the heavens that I had ever known or sensed. He was making room in me *to inhabit me!*

I now saw the Lord in everything; in deep magic and in deep love. The magic was in all living things; even in inanimate objects such as the bricks of a house, curtains, furniture, in armchairs waiting for people to sit in them, ready to hold them and comfort them. I saw mysticism and love enfolded in all things, deep and dreamlike, fairy-tale enchantment, bespangled with stardust.

There was also the magic of human love. A very romantic person will often question why they are so deeply romantic. Why they adore love songs. And now I discovered from true mystics, often Zen or Christian Buddhists, which sounds a contradiction but isn't, that deep romantic love between man and woman is one of the greatest joys of our Lord. Again I seemed to have known this from when I was small. Love in all its forms is beautiful.

Some of my prayer pictures had had a deeply romantic content. I had been surprised by this, and at the time I had questioned it. In fact, I had questioned lots of things that I later found to be right. I was always afraid of doing the wrong thing, or putting things in the wrong context, or placing too much emphasis on things that were unimportant. I was fearful that I would offend my Lord, and not do justice to His work. Not until later did I learn to trust my own judgement.

My Lord taught me many things in prayer at this time; sometimes in pictures, but more often in the spoken word. It was lovely; oh how I greeted Him when we met; my joyous heart leaped out of my body to meet Him, and His heart came towards mine, and we embraced. It was so beautiful. I often wished that I could write with my pen dipped into a special inkpot of honeyed words for you, for ordinary words will not serve.

One might have expected our meetings to have been very reverent, hushed, and full of wise sayings. But no, they were not like this at all. Sometimes I sang love songs, or even jingly songs that amused me, to my Lord, and we would laugh together. One day I was feeling quite down in the dumps, and He said something funny to make me laugh. I answered with a popular song; "S'wonderful, marvellous, that you should care for me." And of course it

83

was so true. Anything I sang related to Him and to me; we came together as lovers, and where once I would have hesitated to use these words, I now know that they are right. I had learned that in mysticism this is quite so, for often the writings of medieval saints use these very words. We came together as lovers, and He brought out all the femininity of me, all my womanhood. I'm young again, and glorious in His love. I meet my true love, and we are together forever more.

We talked of many things, but afterwards the words always seemed elusive, and I had to pin them down and record them on tape, to capture them, as I had been asked to do. The elusiveness of prayer releases itself into the spirit; into the knowing. All things, I am told, when goodly thought, are knowing.

Knowing belongs to the world. The world is mantled by the knowing, of love in all its forms. So every good thought you have, or every wish you make unto yourself; that is good. And the good that you wish for people, or kindly thoughts for them, is the goodliness of knowing. And the knowing mantles the world and feeds the world, for we all are nourished by the knowing.

It's getting to know the unknowing that is difficult, the thick fog that surrounds us, and cloaks our Lord from us. We start in the infant's class, where we are only allowed to see a little of Him at a time. Gradually we learn and progress, until finally we reach the senior class, with the great teachers of the world; when we know more. The knowing takes a long time.

One morning, on feeling the love of my Lord, I said to Him:

84

"I can only feel a little of the love You have for me; it is so immense. It is rather as though I am given just a teaspoonful of this immense loving. Even a teaspoonful of Your love is so immense that my body becomes alive, and full, and reaches beyond the boundaries of flesh. I grow immense with it, and that is with just a teaspoonful. I feel that the giant eternity of Your love is being held back, for if it was all given to me, I fear I would explode, for I could not possibly contain such immensity of love. One would have to die, and live with You forever to know that, so we must all know this little, and yet such immense amount of love on a teaspoon."

"Give them honey," You said to me once. "Give them honey, Dorothy. They are mostly sad people, lost and bewildered. Even those who appear happiest on the outside are dreadfully lonely inside. Give them honey!"

And You showed me a great honeypot, full of all good things, and dipped the spoon in. And as I meet people who are lonely and disillusioned, bereaved and sad, and have all sorrows and pain, I dip the spoon into the honeypot for them, and give it to them, that they may be comforted and warmed, for this is no ordinary honey. It is fortified by the spirit, and is greatly warming and rewarding, comforting and enjoyable. It can bring laughter after tears, I have found. So I give them honey. I take generous helpings for myself too. On low days, I need it.

Getting back to the unknowing, or knowing the unknowing: it sounds confusing, doesn't it? It is confusing, but you can see through it when you try, if only you know the right way to go about it. It is like the difference between high and deep. I asked my Lord about this. I said

85

to Him:

"I'm paddling in some vast seas here, Lord. They are dark and deep. How can they be high when they are deep?" He told me:

"Stand on the bottom of this deep, dark ocean of my love that you see, and look upwards. As you look, there is the height that stretches on unending. So there above is your height of me, and there is your depth of me, and there is your width of me, all this great dark sea that you see."

So I paddled at the edge of this deep dark sea.

"Can you feel the knowing creep through you, from your paddling foot?" He asked. "Can you feel it?"

And I could. It spread up to my heart, and there was the knowing that shall be taught. It comes from the heart, not the mind. The mind contains ordinary things, such as "Is it sheet-changing day? What shall we have to eat? What Mrs Brown said today! I must go to the dentist. I must weed the garden. I must cut some flowers for the vase." All things like that are in the mind, but the heart swells with longing and loving and yearning. I said again to my Lord:

"In the magic of Your presence, and the fullness of You, and the immense love that You bring to me, I feel like a silly young girl, when I want to be fully mature and full of love too. I come to you feeling vaguely silly and shallow, when I want to be so deep with love and knowledge. The word many mystics use is tinny, and I think that is a wonderful word, for I feel like an empty drum; if you tapped on me, I would just go 'bong,' for there doesn't seem to be much inside me. But when I look deep within me, yes, there is a lot there. Do you get tired of this silly young girl, Lord, primping and prancing in front of You? I often feel like a wanton, a strumpet I called myself this morning."

A strange idea. A strumpet that lays in bed and does nothing but read, and watch television, and listen to radio, and talk to her friends and visitors and family. A strange strumpet indeed. But a strumpet in the sense of wilfulness or wantonness; I am always wanting something. I love clothes, I love colours. I love the brightness of fabrics and all pretty and joyous things. I love ornaments and jewellery. I love the deeper meanings of things. I seem to want, want, want more nearness of Him, and I want Him to manifest Himself to me in so many ways, in signs and wonders. Want want want! A goodly dressed strumpet. But He laughed, and I knew it was perfectly all right to be called that.

We laugh a lot, my Lord and I. We have many jokes between us. That is the joyful side of it. But let us turn now to the other side of it. The serious, sad and dark side of it.

I have seen Christ on His cross, His dear face haggard, with pain bitten deep into it, and white where the blood had been sucked from it by the devouring, ever-present agony. He was enduring the unendurable for us. At the time I was questioning Him about unbearable pain on earth, and how difficult it is to sustain a spiritual energy that must go forth into the world, when locked in our own prison of pain, whatever it might be.

This is when I see my Lord in desolation. And yet it is when I see Him during desolation that the real strong spirit of my Lord within me comes forth, and the real strength of love. Love that has no boundaries, and is for ever and ever. He was on the cross when He told me about the jar of honey, and to give people all the sweet things and the good

87

things, to give them hope and to lift them up. This is such true teaching, for when I am very, very down, and feel numb, and cannot even pray properly, this is where I need someone too, to help me, and to draw on the knowing.

But there is hope, even in the darkest times of despair. We hunger and yearn, and feel no answer. We actually feel no God at this time. Yet in our hearts we know He is there. We know it, but are quite unable to communicate with Him, or feel His generosity to us until the desolation lifts just a little, and a tiny ray of light penetrates such darkness. When this happens, the darkness recedes, oh so slowly, until at last we are able to come out of the deep despair, from desolation into consolation again. Back into the joy of our Lord where everything is fine and bright and beautiful, loving and laughing again.

When one is in desolation, it seems to last forever; a deep, depressing downward spiral into nothingness. Nothingness is hard to describe, and at first I did not understand it. Then at last I learnt what nothing is. Nothing is God.

This must sound strange to people who have not experienced it, but it is an answering of the inner self, the knowing self. My physical eyes were opened by a book, which showed me what my spiritual eyes had seen for a long time, for as I read about the nothing, I realized that I had always known about it. The nothing is a great void, God's time; the great spaces of eternity, where nothing seems to exist. And yet of course the nothing is filled with something, and that something is God the Father, the Godhead, the fountainhead of life. The nothing is filled to the brim with all things, from the planets and stars to the smallest creatures upon earth, glorious plantations and waters, great seas and gentle streams, mountains and icebergs. All this planning, all this time, the blueprint of it all, is in the nothing. When we, in our deepest despair, spiral ever downwards, and go towards the numbness of the nothing, we are actually travelling upwards at that time of seemingly going downwards; we are going upwards towards our Christ. It is sowing the seeds within ourselves, ready for the consolation to come, when renewal and rebirth comes, as it does every time after deepest despair. We come through this turgid blackness into the light, and hope and love and laughter are renewed. But what we don't at first know at that time, is that when going through the darkness we grow tremendously, for we are then in blind faith, for our eyes are closed. They are shut for us; we cannot see in deep despair. So we travel on in the blackness, unseeing, but with faith, eternal faith within us, never letting go, never giving up. It is very difficult, this learning, for it is God's work, and the deepest and most profound part of God's work is not found so much in consolation, but in desolation of the most profound kind. To describe it, I would have to find words to portray God, and this cannot possibly be done, except by God Himself. And even if I could find the words, they would not be in a tongue that we would understand. I know they exist, for they are within me, but as a feeling; a knowing, something more than mere words. We each must find them for ourselves.

So a little hope during desolate times. Spiral downwards slowly into the nothing, and then you have found your profound God, and that is when you really grow. Each time it happens, there is a teaching, and you will come out of it a little wiser than when you went in. It's jolly hard to live with. At such times everything is wrong; nothing makes sense any more but faith, dear faith, and Christ's face looking at you from His cross. Share with Him that time, and then let the nothing begin to work within you, and come out into the light, for although you may not know it, you will have seen His glory even in those darkest times. His face is with you then; you may possibly see Him clearer then than in the lighter times; this often happens. You can only look back at it, and then see through it, and it's true, as though through a glass darkly, you can see things when you are removed from them, and see in its perfection, what has truly happened within you.

We must go on, in pain and despair, but what does it do to us, this wretched physical pain that makes the flesh shrink and the mind shudder under its impact. It is nothing compared to His suffering for us, and yet look what released itself when our Lord finally died in His dreadful torment! As the earth spun on its axis, the light of our Lord's love travelled like some fire around and across the world until it was encircled by the flame of His love. And He had to endure crucifixion for us, and die for us, for it to occur.

This world of ours, encircled by the flame of His love, far outshines any sun when seen with spiritual eyes. This world of ours, where physical pain seems to conquer all, and vanquish all in death, does not conquer, for after death the spirit rises in ecstasy. For pain did not conquer. Ecstasy was the victor. That above all matters; the victory over pain.

Not only in death, but in life too we can have victory over

pain, by standing by all we believe in, all we have faith in, all we have love in; by our Lord, our Holy Father. That is victory over pain. And that in itself, in times of consolation, can bring ecstasy in prayer, lasting ecstasy. Even in the darkest nights, faith and prayer intermingle, while love added to it makes it wildly intoxicating, and you can live in this spiritual joy even through the long nights of the spirit.

I know all about the long nights, for I have lived much of my life in them. Night is often the stronger time in which to reap our rewards, for true knowing comes in the night. In the light there are so many distractions; colours and friends and cups of tea, laughter and gossip, but in the darkness of the night, there are none. That may sound gloomy, but it is not meant to be. Silence can also be called night, and this can take place during the day. For it is in a state of mind that this occurs, that this comes to us; a state of deeper feelings, as the layers of consciousness are gradually peeled away.

Deeper and deeper we go as layer upon layer of consciousness and outer awareness is stripped away from us. Deeper and deeper yet we go, until we reach that part of us which is night, where all is quiet and dark and peaceful. It is as though our physical body is a house into which we retire, pulling the curtains and shutting the doors, to sit quietly within its depths. Or even better, our own temple, for we are going to meet our Lord.

In the daytime I wear a mask. I put it on to greet friends, and I try to wear it for my family, for I do not want them to see the face behind it. It is not always easy to do this; sometimes the mask slips a little, and those closest to me

91

see what lies behind it. But not casual friends and acquaintances. For them I keep it firmly tied in place. It is a smiling mask; a jovial mask, a mask of sweet friendship. A clever mask, constructed by me when I was very small, and it has grown with me. You see, when you have a smiling mask, others don't see the pain behind it, and so they are not troubled by my pain. This means that they can tell you of their problems freely, and with a clear conscience. Only special people see behind the mask when it is allowed to slip a little.

But when I am deep in my temple, with my Lord, and there are only soft candles glowing, my mask is taken off and set on one side. We can sit and talk, my Lord and I, with my true countenance showing. He knows it dearly, and love flows between us. This love is a tangible thing, which I can bring back from the deep night into the daylight when I open doors and windows, and pull aside the curtains of my temple to let the sun in again. Do not shun the darkness of the night. Learn to love it, learn to feel it, learn with all your deepest and most profound senses, to feel it. It can give back to you the most amazing things, the most amazing happenings.

In the darkness of the night you will hear the silent music, music that runs through all eternity, and through us, as though we were not there. It is the harmony, the rhythm of all things. It is preludes, fandangos, great symphonies of joy, all things that are in harmony. One of the strongest of all is our heartbeat, which keeps us upon this earth. Another is the prayer that is throughout this world twenty-four hours a day, never ending, never ceasing. Prayer surrounds us all, for even in our sleeping time, someone on the other side of the world is saying a prayer. Hundreds of thousands of people are praying every minute. The silent music is life, and awareness of life, and the rhythms of life, and all things beautiful and loving are contained in this music. So in your darkness, listen quietly, for it comes at such times, the silent music of the night.

A new day begins, and the silent music becomes revelation. This renewal in prayer always happens, and one morning, talking to my Lord, I asked Him about the world's imperfections.

"Lord, why in this time are there imperfections? I am so often asked this question, and can never give people a really satisfactory answer. For example, when they sorrow for, and feel so deeply about handicapped children, or starvation in Africa, or the sadness and cruelties we see throughout the world. And bereavement sometimes turns people away from God. I meet many people with problems who look to me for an answer. God talks within me and helps me find an answer, but it is not always satisfactory, for how can we know the real works and the real mind of God?"

I told Him how difficult it is, and He knows it all so well. Of my incapacity, that doesn't get easier, and my having to rely more and more on others as time passes. The indignity of being washed by others perhaps, or having them empty my commode, which is always the horror of horrors for me. I have never grown used to it. In answer, I was shown my feet, ankle deep in that dark deep sea, in the void of the nothing. The voice spoke to me:

"In this void there is much learning. The earth was made imperfect, as we all know. God could have made a perfect earth for us to live in. Take the tree!"

I looked, and saw the tree. It was a perfect apple tree, growing in perfect lawns, with not a blade of grass out of place. Its trunk was beautiful, without gnarls, and its branches curved in absolute harmony, with nothing twisted or stunted. Each leaf was beautifully marked, shining, and straight, with no curling, while the fruits that hung from the branches were magnificently formed, curving green and red, the colouring just right, with no blemish or worm. So there stood this perfect tree. Then the voice said:

"Imagine you are all perfect. Every one of you is perfect. It is a perfect world. Where now do you get your feelings? Where now is your deep love, conquering all sorrows?"

This was all so true. I went deeper into my consciousness, into the dark awareness of prayer, the awareness of being together, my Lord and I, and I questioned on. In our England the soil is rich, and the climate is right, and all good things grow from the earth. I then saw the barren lands of Africa. The sun was hot and unrelenting. There is little water. No goodness can grow there. I saw clearly the imperfection. It is still hard to understand the reason why, but I felt I had a glimpse of it.

We are all different, white skins, brown skins; all living on this imperfect earth. Yet we are blessed beyond comprehension. Mankind stands on this earth, feet firmly planted, and reaches with eager hands to the stars. Yes, we were given that too, the hunger for the stars, while there are times on earth when we are moved by certain things. For me it is music, and for a while I am transcended out of my body by a particularly beautiful piece of music, and lifted up into the heavens among the stars. Or a man and woman falling in love; a mother and baby, we see fractions of such love, and are uplifted by them. Kiss the face of God. It is magnificent, and words cannot describe it. How we all love.

We all have treasures buried deep in the rubble of our subconscious. Tear away the rubble, the nuisance and the anger, the indignity. Let them flow away from you, and dig deep to find the true treasure. It is there. We are seekers after truth, treasure, love of God, and we find the most precious and lift it in our arms. Eyes bright, we begin to understand; we know a little of the unknowing.

I said earlier that my Lord made room in me to inhabit me. This took years of scouring and cleansing me. He set fire to me, burning me with longing, and with hopeless frustration when I failed miserably to accomplish my task. So elusive was He at times that I wanted to pick up my crucifix and throw it across the room in fury.

Often in my prayers He passed by, with me unknowing. I only saw the edge of a fleeting shadow across the blinding light of His Blessed Son. I smelt the fragrance; I knew it was Him, and I was up and after Him again. I entered deep down in prayer, peeling away layers and layers of awareness, and sought Him in the deepest darkness, where there is no light at all. But because I desired Him so much, there was no fear, for the overriding fear was of not finding Him at all, and being lost forever.

In this I was heartened by the words of St Teresa of Avila. "Be courageous my daughters," she said. "Have courage my daughters." Feeling myself to be a daughter of St Teresa, I entered fully into the chase, that was to be partnered by my Lord God right the way through, although

He was in heavy disguise, and appeared as the nothing.

Great empty vistas; an enormous void of darkness; anguish and heartache awaited me. Often I felt a dismal failure in spirit. I searched the hot arid desert wastelands, and the icy coldness of the outer reaches of space where man does not dwell, nor dare to enter. But I entered it. It was so cold; far colder than the polar regions of earth, for this was the coldness of the questing spirit, seeking the ultimate fulfilment of the Living God. In the wastelands, where there was nothing to eat or drink, I sat and wept, then fell asleep. Waking, I felt too disheartened to continue, feeling that there was no more journey to be had; that I had reached the end of my quest. There was nothing else. I deserved no more than this, and on my knees would praise Him for the little that I had, only to find that I had been given a different path; a different way to seek Him. Renewed energy was given me.

One morning, as I entered the deep awareness, I said to Him: "Lord, I wish to see inside myself, to see if I have made any space for you yet."

For this was my desire more than anything. To look inside myself. And this was granted. For my prayers themselves, infused with vision, were shown to me, and the eye of my soul allowed me to see an image, draped for me, that my human recognition would understand.

I knew how the Sorcerer's Apprentice must have felt, doing something terribly daring, but at the same time, undeniably sweet. With great temerity, and with many fearful looks over my shoulder, like a small child peeping into a wizard's cauldron, I tiptoed over to the edge of myself.

At first I saw only the edge of myself. Little more than a thin waver of bright light, such as one sees during an eclipse of the sun, when all is not quite black; just a thin light before the final diminishing takes place. I saw this thin, fragile, wavering light, luminous in the dark, and peered inside.

And there I beheld my interior, my interior life. It was immense. How could I have spread out so widely, have become so enormous, that I had captured inside me the very heartland of the cosmos. The whole universe was spread out there. Peeping over the edge of myself, I gazed into an infinite being inside me. It was full of ... nothing! And therein was the Living God.

It was too much for me to grasp. I was dumbfounded; witless. Yet at the same time I felt a gratitude beyond all, an immense giving to my Father, my endless gratitude stretching out to Him. It seemed so small a thing to give; gratitude for life, for living. The blessedness of it all.

But that's what it was. All I had to stake I had given. I had thrown my chips on to the gaming table. I had dared, with my very soul at risk. That was the pledge I had made, and He had answered me thus. I was completely overawed; and full of reverence and devotion for Him. Love swept over me, its power annihilating me, diminishing me, tearing me asunder, scattering me to the four winds of the universe, among the stars and the great galaxies. I was a living part of every entity.

In this enormity of what I had seen and become, how could I ever get myself back together again? How could I reform myself, and return to being a mere mortal again, having danced the dance of the universe with our most

97

Holy Father, the Eternal Lord? How was I to recover my senses and come back?

For what seemed an eternity I waited, slowly, oh so slowly recognizing the pathway back into my human form. Gradually the threads wove again, and the things that make each of us special knitted together, through all the layers, to become me. Finally I arrived back in my familiar bedroom, squinting against the bright daylight which settled around my eyelids, allowing me once more to open my earthly eyes. Once more I was me, but now knowing what lay in my interior. I had glanced into my own soul, and my spirit rejoiced at such grace.

Such was the treasure buried in my fields of awareness. Journeys through the ice-cold places and the arid deserts, into the deep, deep dark. Stubbing my toes on the hard rocks; blasted by heat and chilled beyond measure by cold, with the deep shadows lengthening. The frustrations and angers had all been rewarded, but first I had had to tread through the dreadful desolation; to endure the stripping and wounding, the unbearable agony of shouldering the cross and walking with it, finally to find myself pinned on it and crucified.

The tremendous burden of taking on oneself the worldly sins of mankind, the immense sufferings of the world; taking them all and carrying them, accompanied by the crucified Lord Christ. Jesus, the historical Lord, speaking now through the pages of the sacred Bible. Speaking to me clearly.

"I am with you. I am the same as your flesh. I tear and hurt and bleed the same as you. I am your shadow companion on the cross. At my pleasure and my time, I shall lift you down from your cross, and henceforth raise you. Your spirit shall ascend with mine into the triumphant heavens, to be fully embraced by our Father, the most Holy Lord God. We shall go with Him, and be in His heavenly mansions, His Soul forevermore. Until then, when at His command your soul leaves your body, His owning of you shall join in complete transformation of the Kingdom to come. Your heavenly home awaits. Meanwhile its sweet perfumes reach you, leading you the dance of the deepest desire. You have survived all, and passed with merit."

And so I am blessed beyond all comprehension. All that was given to me, from the moment of birth, was here now. And I at last, suffused by rapture, lifted up in divine love, knew at last the Living God.

# CHAPTER 5

# Illuminations

Often over the next few years I was shown strange and wondrous things in what I now came to call illuminated prayer. These experiences were in some ways similar to the prayer pictures, but subtly different, for the learning content was greater and more direct. No longer did I have to pore over the meaning in the picture; its meaning was there in front of me. I was now ready for this new style of learning, which I had not been before. Whereas I had always felt impelled to record the prayer pictures, I only rarely committed these later illuminations to tape, but the memory of them remains as clear as if they happened yesterday.

One thing that puzzles many people is the lot of mankind in the days before our Lord Jesus walked the earth. We who have lived since have had the benefit of His teachings, but they did not. Nor of course did many people who came after Him, for His Gospels were slow to spread, and are still not universal. What chance had they of salvation?

We know that our ancestors worshipped all manner of strange gods and goddesses. Celestial deities of the sun and moon. Mighty gods of the underworld, the earthquake or the seas; and lesser spirits of trees, lakes or rivers. Gods of wisdom, of the harvest, and of fertility; of rebirth and renewal; of death and destruction. Gods of the hunt, of war, and of the making of things. Every natural feature, every human activity and attribute had its god or goddess. Why was this, and where did they all come from? Were they merely the products of superstitious minds, or the inventions of a cynical priesthood, seeking to grasp and keep power over the people? While there can be little doubt that both these last factors played a part, could there have been something more? Could they in fact have been part of the divine plan?

Once more I sought an answer, and once more I received one. It lay deep down in the psyche, where all treasures are hidden. We have to dig for them and find them, and bring them anew to the light of the world.

The old gods existed many thousands of years before my birth. They are all trapped in the cosmic awareness, the cosmic consciousness—the collective consciousness that Carl Jung and other great philosophical teachers have written about. I, without knowing it, was treading the same path as they. This is not meant to be boastful, for, humble before my Lord in all things, I took the path in all humility. And I experienced to the full that cosmic consciousness really does exist.

Many times on entering these deep dark recesses of the psyche, I discovered things inside me that I hadn't realized were there. How could I possibly have known? But in deep prayer, one lets all the outside world go and disappear, so that one becomes a total channel for the Holy Father, my

Lord God, to communicate His wishes and His desires, and His might. In the long hard road that you must travel to get to the inner sanctum, to the throne room, you are beset and besieged by many strange sights and adventures; some so strange that you actually wonder at and doubt them. But on being reassured always that this is the correct way, you go on again. It is a quest and a journey, and a hard one at that. The prize is not to be won easily. This is how the search for the Holy Grail must have seemed to our ancient counterparts, the knights of old, when they went in search of the great treasure of our Lord.

I saw such strange things on my journeys, many of which were non-Christian. I had never thought to encounter the old gods, and these experiences often greatly puzzled me, causing me to question my Lord about them.

"Is this right my Lord, that I should see things that are pagan?" But always I was reassured, "Yes, this is the way."

God comes in many facets, and many guises. We are unable to understand just that God IS. With no face for us to see, nor form, He is very hard to envisage. Failing to understand, we could easily put Him back in a drawer, out of sight.

To make Him more understandable: He was in the past divided into many gods or deities, each one representing a different aspect of Him. Many have said to me: "You are speaking of gods instead of the One God, the Almighty Creator. Surely this is pagan teaching?" But it must not be forgotten that long before you and I entered this world, mankind followed the pagan way of progress. This path provided the first enlightenment, showing us how to reach God.

I have been shown the coming of man upon the earth. It is all there, buried deep in the psyche, and as you go down into it, stripping away the layers of consciousness, you may reach these times, times even before man. I thought that I would see steamy jungles and swampy places, and of course they did exist. But to my absolute delight, I also saw flowers and fruiting trees, which were there upon Mother Earth even before mankind.

I saw prehistoric humanity depicted as one person. It was night, and myriad brilliant stars shone in the dark sky, against which strangely shaped trees and bushes were blackly silhouetted. All was still. Then in the deepest shadows, something moved. As it came forward, my eyes made out its shape, and I saw that it was man. Apelike in appearance, shoulders hunched forward, but definitely man. As he emerged into the open, I sensed an immense loneliness about him. He was alone in the world, with no one to turn to for help; for solace, for comfort.

Before him was a puddle. He shambled towards it and knelt to drink, stretching out his cupped hands to the water. As he bent forward, he saw reflected on the surface of the puddle, the luminous orb of the bright moon. Carefully, reverently, he dipped his hands into the water, and for an instant he held the moon image, in all her resplendent glory, in his palms. He looked up and gazed long at the real moon in the heavens, then down once again to its reflection in the water. Again he looked up, and the stirrings of awareness of something beyond his knowing entered him. With this his loneliness fled, and I felt him attune himself for the first time with God the Creator.

We must travel far and wide through ourselves to find

great truths, and when we find them, we must have courage enough to confront them. Often they appear alien, and at odds with all we have been taught. This is difficult when at first we cannot believe them. The temptation is always to say no, this cannot be so; I cannot accept this, and I reject it; I shut it out.

That is not the way. We must be brave and open doors. The test is always to have a feeling of rightness about a thing; always to get a feeling of rightness. And when we have finished, and laid a meditation or a journey behind us, we must feel good about it. Anything that leaves a bad aftertaste, or a frightening feeling that stays with us, must be discarded. Anything that grows stale and loses its flavour must be put aside. The right way leaves us feeling good, and ready to progress further, happy with the world and happy within our own skins. This is the right way to travel into the unknown. We are travelling into the God of the Unknown.

The journey down into the self is long and arduous, and there are dragons to be overcome at every level. The dragons are our own faults; ignorance, greed, fear and selfishness. They guard the caves of the inner treasure, and will try to keep us at bay, and prevent us from progressing further. But our virtues will come to our aid. Endurance and tenacity and endeavour will armour us, and in our hand will be the sword of valour.

Confront the dragons with faith and innocence, humility, and trust in our Lord. Descend from cave to cave, ever seeking the light. You will be beset, and turned back many times. Every time this happens your faults and your virtues will be shown you. Overcome the faults, and enhance the virtues, until you come to the antechamber, where you will be robed to enter the throne room.

There are many sacrifices to make along the way. It costs a great deal to follow this path. Again this is in the ancient teachings; the holy books and scriptures. They all say, put down your tools, put down your pleasures, and follow me!

\* \* \* \* \*

One morning I entered into and became part of the great fields and greenery which cloak the earth's surface. I was part of the spirit of the green and the red berry tree, of the great sacred oak, and the mistletoe; the only hope of winter. The creatures of earth too, I entered into; all the wild dear things of our Holy Father; rabbits and deer, hedgehogs and mice; and birds of the air; from fledgelings to eagles, all rejoicing, and I rejoiced with them. The domestic animals too; horses and cows; sheep and chickens; placed upon earth for us to gaze upon in infinite joy, to use, and of course, to feast upon. We should hold them so dear unto Him. All are His beloved creations. And among these things, very much alive and dancing his dance across the surface of the world, was the god Pan, revered by our ancient ancestors. His appearance I cannot describe, for he was a part of the whole; part of every living thing, even as I was. I had become both the worshipped and the worshipful.

On other occasions I saw the wine god, Bacchus. He was full of enjoyment and merriment, lord of all the pressed fruitings of the earth, made into delicious wine, and bringing the wine of the Blessed Sacrament. There too was the mother earth goddess, she of the many names, of abundant giving and fecundity; of renewal and rebirth in all things. The pregnant earth, always giving an abundance of her food and wine. Our ancestors, living in harsher times, celebrated these things to the full with revelry and rejoicing, in a way that we no longer know. We, distracted by our domestic comforts, have lost this. We have lost the great rampaging spirit of earth; the fullness of it; the great giving of it, and the taking from it.

Nor was this all. I was to hear strange words thunder through me. Odin, the great Norse god. Odin! Odin! The great cry of the Vikings that is in our blood. This is what we are made of. The great cry in the blood, the great and powerful god of the warrior is in us still. I often feel the strength of the warrior god arise in me. The immense power of Odin, that was so real to our ancestors; so strong they could almost taste him.

Other gods too clamoured in on me; all to be rejoiced and come together as a complete whole when the Christ Child was born, blessing them with His birthing, making all things pre-Christian become Christian, baptizing them in His Becoming the Son of Earth and the Immortal Heavens. In Him the heavenly spirit of our Lord God had arrived, blessing all that came before Him, and making all things right.

All these gods and goddess are embroidered on the hem of the gown of our Lord God, like delicious and dazzling gemstones. As He passes by, and brushes earth with His presence, we see the wonders of the hem of His gown. Here are the great gods and goddesses of Olympus: Zeus and Apollo, Persephone and Aphrodite, and so many

many more. Isis and Osiris of ancient Egypt, Vishnu and Shiva of the Hindus, all are there; shining brightly, all are woven into a dazzling tapestry on the very hem of His gown. I give grateful thanks to my Lord for showing me, and allowing me to see such revealing of the hidden treasures.

But while all such revelations are illuminating, some have to be bought, and the price is high. On one of my interior journeys, I encountered Nemesis, the great goddess whose purpose is to make all things right. It was a fearsome experience. Once more setting off down through the layers of consciousness, I arrived... I know not where.

* * * * *

The fog swirled around me. Dark grey, dense and choking, it was almost thick enough to drown in. It constantly ebbed a little way before rolling back in again, like some unearthly tide. Designed to keep all comers at bay with its suffocating intensity, it guarded the forbidden place, stifling those who, in idle curiousity, dared to enter. I stood completely still. I dared. The fog swirled ever more fiercely, radiating waves of fear, trying to repel me. It took my utmost courage to withstand it. No idle curiosity, mine; I knew that I must be there; that something was about to be revealed to me.

Time ceased to exist. Forever I seemed to stand there in this hostile fog. The fear built up, and began to border on sheer terror of what was to come. Quaking, I determined to know what lay behind it. This something mattered more to me than my frail life.

107

Gradually the fog began to thin. While it knew of my fear, it also knew that I would sacrifice my life to see what was to come. Slowly it dispersed, and I emerged into light. Not a brilliant light, it had no apparent source, but was all-pervading, such as one finds on a cloudy day. But there were no clouds.

The ground I stood upon was beaten earth. This was symbolic; I was a child of Earth, I was made of earth. I gazed out on... nothing! To look at absolute nothing, a void that goes on and on for eternity, is very hard to describe, just looking into daylight without form or being. I felt the familiar blend of trepidation and daring as the fog finally vanished, clearing the way for me to advance.

It was then that I first heard the voice. Deep, yet genderless, it did not echo, but sounded as though it ought to. A voice with a dimension different to the human voice, with a greater range, somehow rounder and vaster. I gained the impression that it was modulating its immensity of tone to suit the human ear. It came from no visible entity; it belonged to the fog, to the vastness.

It came from no particular direction, but seemed to resonate all around me.

"You dare to enter this place!"

The tone was utterly commanding, making me even more aware that I was an Earthling; made of earth, and feeling earth under my bare feet. I felt that I was a lesser being, held in a sort of amused contempt. Yet behind that contempt, the voice was charged with menace, with the underlying "you dare". It spoke again.

"Show me your worth!"

This was thundered forth. The amused contempt was

gone, replaced by overt threat. Thus would a bullying adult try to frighten a waif, and I felt very much a waif by now.

I became aware that I was wearing a long, rough, dun-coloured garment; half coat, half robe. At the command "Show me your worth," I dug deep into the large pockets. Hidden in the corners of them I found coins. They were very small, less than the size of a thumbnail, and few in number, perhaps five. They were, however, gold, and imprinted on them was a strange text, or maybe a password. They seemed to know each other; the coins and the voice. This reassured me that I would be accepted. Another command came.

"Throw down your worth!"

As I dropped the coins on the ground, I remember feeling that they were pathetically small, both in value and in number. I was ashamed of them. Totally inadequate, I felt that I had no right to be there, but somehow the coins had given me that right. They were a token of my humanity; of what I was.

The voice seemed to know this, and as they fell softly to earth in front of me, the thundering ceased as it saw the worth. But my dreadful feelings of shame and inadequacy persisted. Shame of being human to enter there while I was still mortal. It would have been better had I been dead, and gone from earth. It would have been easier for me to have been there; I would have been more at home with the voice. I was ashamed of my mortality, of the lowliness of earthly people. The flesh itself is of such poor quality. It gives us our heaviness, our weight of sin; our selfishness and greed; all the things that belong to earth, all the sins of

109

the flesh.

These feelings flashed through me, suffusing me with shame as I gazed down at my pathetic coinage. I was of very little worth to dare to come to this sacred place. But the voice obviously accepted my value, otherwise I would have been cast out, in the full biblical sense, like so much discarded rubbish.

The small gold coins shone dully at my feet. They were grouped closely, as if to emphasize their fewness. In the angles of the strange inscriptions clung tiny pieces of earth, as though my mortality was somehow stuck to the coin. But on seeing them, the voice grew silent.

I then felt impelled to walk forward, towards the nothingness, towards the void. I stepped over the coins, leaving them behind. As I did so, the light changed. It darkened, and began to build up into a wall ahead of me. The wall appeared to have no limits, and was made of dense cloudy matter. It had neither door nor gate, but I knew that I was to be allowed to pass through it. Very dark grey, it was not of earthly stuff, but appeared to be made of fog even denser than that which I had encountered earlier. It was an unearthly barrier, which as I approached, accepted me. I passed into it.

I had expected to pass through the wall into something else, but instead I was enveloped by it. I had entered the threshold of Nemesis herself, although at that time I had no idea who she was. She was hard to describe. Imagine if you can a goddess in dark veils or robes all swishing around, with her at the centre. What had seemed to me to be a wall was the outside of her robes. These were made of a dense dark cloudy matter, which I was later told was cosmic dust. I had entered Nemesis through her robes.

Unlike the original fog, the cloud gave no feeling of suffocation because I had been accepted, and allowed in. I still trembled with fear, because there remained a feeling of immense menace within the cloud. It was a fearful place, even though the life-threatening feeling had gone, but still I wanted more. I wanted to reach the throne room where the goddess dwells. The words came to me now: "she who dares."

The dark cloud once more started to swirl, as it did in the beginning. Within Nemesis one enters a different dimension to that of Earth. The great cloud is how she appears to mortal eyes. This was how I saw her.

Great waves washed against me. Nemesis had neither face nor form; she was like an ocean. An angry ocean, angry at my being allowed to enter. There was no welcome here. Dark grey waves of power buffeted against me as I walked forward, pressing against them, resisting their dreadful anger.

As the waves of power broke against me, colours started to appear, colours flickering briefly against the grey. Such vibrant colours, saffron yellow and orange, swift lightning flashes to show me the spectrum of power. Then a new colour showed ahead; not flashing or flickering, but steady. A dull pink, which on my approach grew rapidly in intensity, turning to dark red, which I first took to be fire. It was not fire, but liquid. I was entering a liquid place now, and I knew instantly what it was, mentally and physically, in my earthly dimension.

It was human blood. For an instant I felt a flash of extreme terror as the blinding knowledge of it was given

111

me. It was an ocean of human blood. I was entering the blood of all mankind from the beginning of time. I was in it; I was of it; I was surrounded by it. I had entered into an earthly dimension of human sacrifice. There was no earth beneath my feet, I was suspended in it. I became a mere corpuscle of it, losing my human self, although I was allowed to retain my human perceptions.

Everything to do with my acceptance and admittance was grudging. The buffeting of the waves continued, but by and by this movement changed to round and round, gathering momentum until it became a whirlpool, taking me with it. I was no longer walking forward. Its own immense power was taking me. Nemesis is made of human sacrifice, both forced and voluntary, from human sacrifices to ancient gods, to the incredible self-sacrifices made by men for their fellows. Nemesis is the sum of all the immense giving of humanity.

I was pulled down into the vortex, round and round, deeper and deeper, into the very soul of Nemesis, into the heart of her creative force. I realized that I was in the presence of a living goddess. No goddess conjured up from cheap paperbacks or dusty museum tomes, nor yet an idealized goddess from ancient history, but living, pulsating. I could feel the very energy, the arterial flow of her. This was the perception of one small corpuscle in the heartflow of Nemesis.

Full perception was now granted me; wondrous images as though from an Alice in Wonderland tunnel. Pictures formed within the flow of blood; pictures of all mankind. I saw them clearly; prehistoric man, times before prehistoric man, the dust destined to become man. The beginnings

112

and origins of all things. The divine plan, set deep in the heavens. The plan conceived by God, the Holy Creator of all things in heaven and earth. This grand design was begun long before Nemesis herself, to prepare for earth and for mankind. Both were lovingly planned. Mankind was designed first, then the Earth for him to stand upon.

The huge power of Nemesis stretches deep into the cosmos, blood red in the centre, and angry grey on the outside of her swirling mantle. She girdles Earth with her strength. Her purpose is to right the wrongs of mankind. For this she was created. The wrongs of warfare, of cruelty, of thoughtless and selfish acts; even the simple and unthinking petty unkindnesses we do each other daily. Nemesis is the great righter of such wrongs. She is the goddess of righteousness, and she belongs to God the Creator. Though huge and great to behold, especially to me, at that time the tiniest part of her being, she is but a small facet of Him.

She next allowed me to see the cosmos. I left the swirling vortex. Red gave way to grey as I travelled back through her outer robes, to perceive, with my puny human understanding, the vast map of Earth before she was formed. The plan was unrolled before me, unending, stretching into the void for all eternity. I was lost to describe the magnificence of it. Stars and planets showed through it, but Earth was paramount, the dearly beloved of the Creator. I saw the Son of the Creator, a child. I was permeated by the feeling: My dearly beloved Earth, My world, come for My Son to stand upon.

The dearly beloved Son, our lifegiver, came first of all. There are two meanings here: the Sun of our Earth, and the

113

Son of Earth to bring heaven and earth together, the spiritual and the temporal. And thus they link up, the celestial and the earthly, through Nemesis, the righter of wrongs. She is the Guardian.

Through illuminations such as this, I learned not so much of the old gods themselves, but of their place in the divine plan. For they were all pre-ordained to play their part in the grand design, and to help prepare the way for the coming of the Son. I turned to my books, and there I found affirmation of what I had learned, for this is the true test of learning. Affirmation. Pick up books of saints, and philosophers, and there you will find it. All the things you knew before, revealed and affirmed for you by the greatness of others. Then you know that you are travelling the right path.

I said in chapter 1 that at first I had no human counsel. As a dear priest friend of mine told me later: "You only had God." And how astounding those words were. It was so true. I had only God to show me the way. And while it might be asked who needs more, our puny human selves, enclosed in the physical world, do not always hear His voice clearly. It is at these times that guidance from a fellow creature, someone who has trodden the path before you, someone who has been beset by the same frailties and weaknesses, is valuable. At times, we all need someone to assure us in so many words, "Yes, that is the right way," even if these words come second-hand from the pages of a book.

Often though, in this second phase of my spiritual growing, the messages were more direct. I have spoken of the crucifixion before; I must return to it again, for it is the hinge and hub of everything, the descent into light, in all its majesty.

*     *     *     *     *

I awoke this morning to pain. Unbearable pain, an agony in which I was utterly lost, and which sent all wondrous thoughts flying for their lives before its hideous barbarity. Pain which seemed to fill the whole universe, with no beginning and no end. In my anguish I called out:

"Where are You? Why have You left me? Why do I suffer this so? Why have You gone? Where are You hiding? Lord God, Father, why have You forsaken me? I love You so much." He answered:

"I was here all the time. You cannot see Me, but I am here with you. You cannot hear Me, but I am here with you. You cannot feel Me, for the pain has obliterated all other feeling from you. What you are now is blotting paper. Sop it up. Draw it into yourself. I am here beside you, and you do not know it. But in your not unknowing, I am the knowing. Everything you know and understand and feel seems to be total chaos. Know then that I am the rightful master of chaos. I am the instigator of chaos, for I know where chaos is to lead you. To the ultimate love, and the rebuilding that will come when you are all but totally lost."

Then, quite plainly, I saw Christ dying upon His cross. He was utterly lost in the pain, as I was this morning when I awoke. Like me, he could not see the glory behind it at that time, and called out to His Father:

"Father, Father, where are You? Why have You done this to Me? Why did You allow them to do this to Me?"

Dear Lord, I see the skies grow dark, and darker still as You call out. I stand so close to You; I am the very breath of You. I understand all that You say, all that You feel and do, and why. Why and why; I know why. I see Your Mother, our Holy Lady, kneeling. She cannot see the radiance that is coming either. She sees only the hurt of her son, most dear in all the world to her, and bows to God's wishes and demands. His will is great upon her, as she shares the agony of her son. She is in the dark time. She cannot yet see the glorious light. With her is Mary Magdalen, bowed down, crushed under the ever deepening darkness of it all.

I see the soldiers around the cross too. They have obeyed the commands of their officer, and of the judges. They stand there. Some are jeering, but others feel uneasy. A few are inwardly questioning themselves, although they dare not utter the words. They seem to feel the stirring of pity for this man, denounced by his own people, and look away for shame.

Great clouds gather; the sky is meeting the earth. The wind blows, gently at first, plucking at their cloaks, stirring the still and foetid air that is filled with human suffering. The sun has disappeared, and the clouds grow denser, blotting out the daylight; finally blotting out light itself, until there is just dark, impenetrable dark, unknowing. The very universe holds its breath; eternity holds its breath and waits. All is silent. It is as though the earth had never been born. All is a great void of darkness. Every speck of light has been obliterated.

The only sounds now are the moans of pain from our Lord in His dying on earth. And now the wind grows stronger; it is answering, answering these moans of human torment. At last, at last God's voice is to be heard over this land of punishment. Stronger and stronger it blows, buffeting the cross where our Lord is nailed for all to see. All mockery is gone now; everything is gone, for the wind is raging, with a fury, and an anger not seen upon earth since it first was born. Now the world unseen must be born, and come to life in this deep darkness.

The clouds cannot hold their oppression, and scud away before the terrible storm, fleeing before the coming Lord and allowing light to return. The wind lashes furiously, spending its anger, tearing at the cloaks of the soldiers. They gaze around them with great unease, for they do not know what more is going to happen. They are frightened for themselves at what they have done. What have we done?

Our Christ has died. He is dead, and is now beyond all human torment. He ascends into the majesty of His Father, taking with Him all human pain and suffering forever. The earth cries out; all now is on the very brink of coming alive, for the death has penetrated it, and has crushed it beyond all reason. The light at last; enlightenment is coming to the world, radiance, pursuing every speck of blackness and transmuting it. The Lord lives, the Lord God lives! Long live the Son of God, Christ Jesus. Long shall he reign over heavens and earth, for eternity! He lifts us up, all, all, and carries us forth into a whole new world of his making. We follow gladly, hastening, running towards Him. Absorbed by light we are now transformed. The grace of God is upon us. Alleluia. Our pitiful cries have become joyful, and we rejoice at His most blessed name.

* * * * *

My pain feels better. I have been transformed from an aching tormented woman to an enchanted one. Transformed by His Being, my wounds are cleansed and made whole. One must know pain before one can help others. One must know all things so that one can help others, so that we do not just know and speak of book learning alone. One must be one with the earthly and the heavenly Lord to be able truly to help peoples of the earth. I know that sad and bleak days await me, but at this special time, I can say with total honesty to you, that I am glad. I am glad to be able to do this small thing for our Lord Christ. To give this one small life I have to give. So with this, I say God bless you all, and may this help you on your way, for that is my most desired wish and prayer for you all.

# CHAPTER 6

# Angels round my bed

Whilst on this earth, seek, and ye shall find. Go forth and find. Then while still on earth, know the Cosmic Christ in all His immeasurable beauty. Thus we are taught. But where to look? Some seek Him in church, but while He is everywhere, He is no more in church than in any other place, and rarely is the preaching from the pulpit fire and wine to set our blood racing, but more often milk and sop. Others seek Him in the pages of learned books. I have mixed feelings about books, for I commenced my quest without their aid, and only later was advised to turn to them. In some I found great inspiration, affirmation of many things that I had been shown, and signposts pointing the way. In this they were invaluable. But others my untutored mind found confusing. They seemed to contain much cleverness but little wisdom. The way to God may be found in books, but He Himself is not there. Where next do we seek?

We do not have to look far. He is to be found within us, in the innermost chamber, the chamber that houses the Holy Grail, your soul. In the Arthurian legend, only the most worthy knights achieved the Grail. So one must

119

strive towards making oneself worthy. This is not difficult. It is done by giving up a part of one's time every day to enter the fields and realms of deepest prayer. This does not take long, at first perhaps only ten minutes. Then as you progress, you will go deeper and deeper. Gradually fill your life with prayer, even when you are about your everyday business. This is not as hard as it sounds; it just needs perseverance. The most mundane task can be performed with reverence as an offering. After a while the whole passage of your life will become a giving to our Lord.

Learn to enter contemplative prayer, and when you do so, you will descend through the layers of consciousness. At each level you will find a cave containing a great treasure, each guarded by a dragon. Armed with faith, with humility, love, charity, and above all, innocence, confront and overcome each dragon in turn. Learn, with the Lord's grace, and you will find the ancients speaking wisdom within you, for they are a living part of you. Beset and besieged, you will be turned back many times. When this happens, have patience and persevere. Overcome your faults and enhance your virtues, and eventually you will succeed. When you enter a cave, do not linger, no matter how precious the treasure within may seem. As soon as your human perception grasps it, if only for a second, pass on. For God Himself is being sought, on and on, through this quest, that you will give your life to attain. In each cave you will find another path, leading ever downwards to yet another cave and another dragon, until at last there are no more caves. Beyond the last cave is the antechamber, which guards the throne room, the holy of holies which lies at the very centre of the soul. The inner self is like a great fortress, fiercely guarded. It cannot be entered in idle curiosity. You must make yourself worthy. You must be worthy in order to be admitted.

In all humility I did not think that I was worthy, but after many years, at last I was admitted. In trepidation, I entered the antechamber. It was a very plain room, with bare floors and ceiling, and with one wall only broken by a large double door which led to the throne room. There were no windows and no lamps; the antechamber was lit only by the radiance from an angel.

The angel was a being of incandescent light, robed in colours not known by human eyes. Celestial colours, irridescent, constantly changing and shifting, almost blindingly bright. Our mortal eyes would be melted from their sockets, for they could not take such brilliance, such beauty. Unless they are shielded in some way, angels can only be seen with the eyes of the soul.

The angel robed me before I entered the sacred throne room. First the white garment of Innocence; then the purple cloak of the Reward of Purity. Only by attaining purity on the inward journey can the purple cloak be given, and placed on the mantle of innocence. Thus clad, I stood in the antechamber and looked around me. All was so plain. The only focal points were myself and the angel. I stood before the double door and waited. As I waited, the light in the antechamber increased in intensity, preparing me to enter the throne room, for a quick transition from one to the other would have been too much for me. One must slowly become infused with light before advancing, to make it bearable to cross the threshold into the most Holy.

121

Slowly the great doors opened, and I entered. Passing the last door of all, I entered the Holy Lord God, the Cosmic Christ in all His splendour. At that moment all became clear; all doubts and perplexities were resolved and melted away. All was revealed within me, a living person on earth. The great nourishing began then, although the intimacy was too great, and human vocabulary too limited to describe it.

I brought it back from the throne room; back into everyday life. The great feeding; the great nourishment to be given to the whole earth. I felt then that I was the Holy Eucharist, the bread and the wine, the body and the blood of the living Christ. The veils drew around it again, enclosing the soul, where it burned as some sacred light.

After this sacred journey into the very heartlands of the soul, the centre of the fortress, I came slowly, very slowly back into my human body. It takes a time to gather oneself. At this point you are not of this world, and yet must come back at His command and dictate that you live in the world again. This threading and weaving and gathering back the human body after such a sacred meeting with the inmost part of your soul, is difficult to describe, for the conscious levels are fed back very very slowly. I had left my human body totally behind, and with it the world that we live in. To me, all such things had died and become one of the greater parts of the glory of the celestial blessing. In the slow coming back, I became aware of the pain coming through, and creeping back into me. I became aware of the heaviness of the bone structure, of the functioning organs, all the parts of my physical body. I became aware of the heaviness, and of the duty it performs in holding me to the earth. These things became ever more apparent, although the bed I was lying on had not yet fully materialized. Slowly, slowly my senses returned, and I became aware that I was lying on the bed, which had not quite formed yet. Nor had the room, waiting to welcome me, familiar and dear after all these years of lying in it.

My eyes have not opened yet. The eye itself has to change from the soul's eye, the spiritual eye, the inner awareness eye, up through all the levels to the mortal again. Slowly the earth light reached my eyelids, and I knew that I was coming fast now, back into earthly reality. I opened my eyes, and as I opened them, the ultimate blessing lay around me. I beheld for the first time with my human vision, albeit fleetingly, angels around my bed. They had accompanied me to earth, on my journey back from the soul. Although dazzled by their brilliance, I was overjoyed to see my brother/sister angels all in attendant glory around my bed. Many of them. The human perception of angels, the image that we have of them, had been imposed upon them for me to recognize them for what they were.

I did not see them distinctly. Their images were constantly shifting and moving, as though seen through a heat haze, or through rippling water. The whole room seemed to ripple. They shimmered in wondrous radiance, cloaked in unearthly colours. Their faces, made bearable for my mortal eyes to see, were translucent. I could see through them; see the bedroom walls through them, and all the time their swirling, dazzling robes constantly shimmered and changed colour. They were smiling, and chattering among themselves as they welcomed me back.

123

It was not like earthly chatter, it was in some high-pitched sonic language; radar language, spiritual language, far beyond the range of the human ear. I could not understand what they were saying, but on seeing them, I laughed with such joy. The human tongue is coarse, and unworthy to speak to them, but with a smile in my voice, I said to them:

"I do not understand what you say, and yet I do understand what you say."

They laughed at this, and at my immense joy in their speech which I did not, and yet did, understand.

Angels are here, these exquisite beings are here in our earthly realm, for us to see. They are here to help us, although we are often unaware of them. Cloaked by the Holy Spirit, and given a shape for us to understand, they come to us on earth with the highest of spiritual blessings. They are our silent companions. Only rarely do we catch a brief glimpse of their heavenly servitude to us, for that is what they are; our servants, sent by the Almighty God. They are the messengers, God's go-betweens, constantly to-ing and fro-ing between heaven and earth, Jacob's Ladder. They are always there, and although we cannot see them, we often feel or hear their presence. For our hearts welcome them, and our souls know them, in joyous harmony. Their last service to us is to accompany us at that final moment when we leave this earth forever, and take us to our true love in His heavenly home. Then will we truly dance with angels.

*  *  *  *  *

While I have always said that the way is not easy, I hope in all humility that I have not made it sound too difficult.

The world we live in has many distractions, and these often intrude however hard we try to shut them out, and concentrate on prayer. It is more than seven years since I first entered a picture, yet I still can be distracted. This was brought home to me quite recently.

It was spring. The glorious spring in the garden, outside my patio window. The spring bulbs, the flowering trees and shrubs, all seemed to have blossomed together. They had never been so bright and so gaudy, displaying their wares for me against emerald green grass and leaves. It was as though Persephone herself danced, flaunting herself for my pleasure. The richness of her flaunting kept taking me away from prayer to our Lord, and every so often my eyes would open, to be dazzled by crocus, daffodil, tulip and hyacinth, and the budding beauty of the trees and shrubs, all bejewelled, the array of dancing spring. I called her Jezebel to her face; an entrancing and delightful Jezebel, to steal me away from my Lord like this.

Resolutely I turned my face away from her, only to meet a glad Lord and discover that He transcends all earth's amazing beauty, while the Holy Mother gives Her bounty and holds us in Her arms. For we take in abundance the gifts of earth, and give them back to our Lord in glorious array with our heartfelt, overflowing thanks for the joy of the ever-coming spring.

We live, as mankind has always lived, in imperfect times, with war, famine, and misery stalking the earth. In the beginning, the cosmic dust was shown on the hem of His gown; and at the end, it has been transformed into the dazzling array of the bejewelled Christ on the risen cross, for us to gaze upon and rejoice in for evermore. Now the

Holy Spirit is rising. The shaft of love once more pierces the very soul of our Lord God, and we eat and drink of Him, and become fully one with Him. Our precious Christ is coming, rising triumphant into the future church; God's wondrous church upon earth. I beheld it. A church which shines diamond bright to light the world; a pure crystal church with an enormous graceful spire, reaching from earth to pierce the very heavens. Earth and heaven unite, behold, we are one. The future is bright and clear, and holds great blessings for the Son of God on this earth, and we are of Him. The future is totally blessed, for all generations to come.

AMEN

# Epilogue

Life on earth is a journey into the unknown. For some the journey seems hard, while for others it appears easier. But appearances are deceptive. Although we may know where we want to go, it is far from easy to tell whether we are on the right path. God is beyond our comprehension; as I said before, He is the nothing, concealed in the clouds of unknowing, but all-loving, all-caring. He cared enough to send His Beloved Son to live on earth, and to die a hideous death for our sakes, and in doing so, to light the way for us. When we are lost or uncertain, it is to Him that we must turn.

Our Lord Christ is a sure guide. Pray to Him, talk to Him, talk as you would to your dearest friend, for he is your dearest friend. And as you would for your dearest friend, set aside part of your day for Him. Then listen. Listen carefully. He will answer. If at times He is silent, have faith, for He is always there. It is just that our human condition sometimes prevents us from hearing His voice clearly.

My own journey has lasted more than sixty years now,

and the way has been long and hard; perhaps harder than most. For most of my life I have been an enforced spectator, rarely a player. So much has been denied me. And yet I count myself blessed.

Books of general Christian interest as well as books on theology, scripture, spirituality and mysticism are published by Burns and Oates Limited.

A free catalogue will be sent on request:
**BURNS & OATES Dept A,**
Wellwood, North Farm Road, Tunbridge Wells, Kent TN2 3DR
Tel: (0892) 510850    Fax: (0892) 515903